PREPARING FOR ACCREDITATION

PREPARING FOR ACCREDITATION

OF QUALITY ASSURANCE OF PROFESSIONAL EDUCATIONAL SERVICES

Prof. Satish Kumar Soni

PARTRIDGE
A Penguin Random House Company

To order additional copies of this book, contact
Partridge India
000 800 10062 62
orders.india@partridgepublishing.com

www.partridgepublishing.com/india

Also by Prof Satish Kumar Soni,

1. "Guidelines for Developing Learning Materials", Authors: Prof S.K. Soni and GT Lalla of TTTI Bhopal, Pub: ISTE New Delhi, India & AICTE New Delhi. Ed: 2000 & 01

2. "Information Resource on Education Technology for Technical and Vocational Education and Training" Part –I, Author: Prof SK Soni, published by M/S Sarup and Sons, New Delhi, India, May 2004, 325 A4 size pages.

3. "Information Resource on Education Technology for Technical and Vocational Education and Training" Part –II, Author: Prof SK Soni, published by M/S Sarup and Sons, New Delhi, India, May 2004, 275 A4 size pages.

4. Engineering Graphics, Author: Prof SK Soni, SPS Publishers, Bhopal, MP, India, May 2008,

Dedication:

The book is dedicated to my **dear wife Asha Soni**, **Bhopal, India**, without sacrifices & support of her, this book could not have even perceived. She sacrificed and accepted to live alone for weeks to gather to let me practice quality assurance consultancy work for professional colleges and where I gained insight into the accreditation processes. The book is the result of the lessons learnt during the consultancy work and previous opportunities to implement many small quality improvement ventures in organizations under sponsored quality improvement projects.

Preface

I am a retired professor and started working in the role of a consultant of quality assurance of professional educational services rendered by higher educational enterprises, at a very advanced age of 70 plus years. A satisfying happiness of providing an useful social service to professional fraternity keeps me mentally fit, despite age related physical weaknesses & pains. After two years of active practice of focused national and international accreditation consultancy work, along with the background of previous work of quality assurance in the form of different aspects of quality improvement endeavors: Faculty & staff Development, Design of Detailed Project Reports (DPRs) for funding by World Bank & Govt. of India projects and assisting in implementation/monitoring of Quality Improvement programs, I gained a lot of awareness into the problems and attitudes of stakeholders towards the activities pertaining to quality assurance & improvements in professional educational services within the constraints of resources, in the throat cutting competitive environment and economic pressures of developing countries.

Based on all my past and current experiences, I can state with conviction that for all developing countries including India & Asia, the only option left is improving the quality of all products, services and operational processes, if they wish to recover from their drooping economic scenario in order to improve quality of life of their citizens. This conviction and my old age made me realize that I must return back to the society whatever little knowledge and expertise I could develop through my short life of 45 plus years as technical teacher at NIT, Bhopal, as a teacher trainer, curriculum developer and as an educational technology practice-nor related to technical & vocational education and training (TVET) systems. This book is an attempt to compile all my learning and I wish to leave its further improvements to other professionals and consultants of future.

The ideas & opinions compiled in this book are based exclusively upon the perceptions and inferences of the author during interactions with client faculty & managers of institutes. These ideas do not represent in any way the views or opinions of the accreditation organizations whose quality assurance philosophies have been illustrated as a vehicle of explaining the logical frame work of quality assurance of educational service enterprises. The purpose is to develop academic awareness & general comprehension of the related concepts and processes of the quality assurance, its benefits to client students and service provider institutions/ organizations.

I got motivated from my compelling inner feelings to even venture into self-publishing mode in order to share my experiential information and learning with my dear fellow faculty members.

This book shall be a good refresher for the experts already practicing in the field of quality assurance and shall provide basic guidance to all faculty members who feel related to some extent with the task for performing the task of preparing documents for acquiring, implementing and sustaining NBA, NAAC & IAO accreditation in India or in some other similar developing country who are using accreditation approaches under the umbrella of Washington Accord.

Prof. S. K Soni

Acknowledgement

I wish to acknowledge with thanks the contributions of all the managers and faculty members who had interacted and facilitated me by giving me grand opportunities to work with them and their talented peers, as consultant or quality improvement motivator, in the projects/ assignments related to interpreting the concepts, processes & criteria involved in the preparations for accreditation. NBA accreditation system under Washington Accord is meant for accreditation of individual programs where as NAAC & IAO accreditation is meant for accreditation of the whole institutions. I sincerely express my gratitude to all those persons who did hard work with creativity with me and made their programs and institution to earn certificate of accreditation from their national and international regulatory agencies. Without such a practical experience, it would have been be very difficult to comprehend & compose such a practice oriented book which shall be relevant and useful to institutions of many developing countries and assist in promoting and installing quality assurance in the higher professional educational sector. Without appropriate quality assurance it is futile to imagine that educated graduates can ever contribute their mite in the best interests of their family, community, country and the glob in improving quality of life of one and all.

I acknowledge, with my heart filled gratitude, the affection of all my family members who all the time appreciated and nurtured my desires and sacrificed their happiness to empower me to serve fraternity of technical professional education.

Satish Kumar Soni

Abbreviations

ABET: Accreditation Board for Engineering and Technology, USA
AICTE: All India Council of Technical Education, India
BS: Basic Sciences Courses
ES: Engineering Sciences Courses
GoI: Government of India
HS: Humanities and Social Sciences Courses
IAO: International Accreditation Organization, < www.iao.org >
MBA: Master of Business Administration Program
MC: Mandatory Course
MCA: Master of Computer Applications Program,
NAAC: National Assessment and Accreditation council, http://www.naac.gov.in
NBA: National Board of Accreditation, MHRD, GoI < www.nbaind.org >
OE: Open Electives
PC: Professional Core Courses
PE: Professional Elective Courses
PEO: Program Educational Objective
PG: Post Graduate
PO: Program outcome
PT: Project and training Courses
QIP: Quality Improvement Program
SWOT: Strengths, Weaknesses, Opportunities and Threats
TEQIP: Technical Education and Quality Improvement Program
TVET: Technical & Vocational Education and Training
UG: Undergraduate
UGC: University Grants Commission

Contents

1 Economy and Technical Education....................................21

1.1: Trends in & Status of Technical Education In India.....................21

1.2: Economy, Quality Assurance and Accreditation..........................27

1.3: International Quality Assurance Accords 31

1.4: Regulation of Quality Assurance..33

2 Outcome Based Technical Education 35

2.1: Current Technical Education System in India 35

2.2: Outcome Based Technical Education System (OBTE):.................39

2.3: Performing Swot Analysis of the Department and the Institute.....45

2.4: Evolving Shared Vision, Mission and Values: 51

2.5. Program Educational Objectives (PEOs)......................................56

2.6: Program (Learning) Outcomes (POs)... 60

3 Innovations for Quality Improvement...............................65

3.1: Rationale..65

3.2: Improving Governance 66

3.3: Improving Four Autonomies 68

3.4: Innovative Faculty and Staff Development 72

3.5: Innovative Classroom Learning And Teaching (L-T) Methods 77

3.5.1: The Classroom Seminar Method: 80

3.5.2: The Classroom Demonstration Method 81

3.5.3 Lab & Workshop based Methods: 83

3.5.4: Innovative Micro, Minor and Major
Project Work Experiences.. 84

3.6: Innovations in Students' Assessment 87

3.7: Innovations in Industry- Institute Partnership...............91

3.8: Finishing School and Placement Center 92

3.9: R&D, Entrepreneurship and Consultancy Center.........................93

4 **Curriculum Modifications (To Accomplish POs & PEOs)** 95

4.1: Accreditation Criteria of NBA, India..............................95

4.2: Quality Improvement in Curriculum Implementation 98

4.3: Modifying Curriculum of Affiliating University 100

4.4: Rubrics for Evaluation and Assessment 106

5 **NBA Accreditation of UG Programs**..............................113

5.1: NBA's- Approach to Accreditation for
Engg & Technology Programs 113

5.2: Tips for Creating A SAR: Criteria 1 115

5.3. Tips for Creating A Sar: Criteria 2:
Program Outcomes (PO) (150) 132

5.4: Tips for Criteria-3 142

5.5: List of Records Files & Exhibits for
showing evidences during inspection 148

5.6: Important Questions ror Managers, Faculty and Students; 152

6 Accreditation of Diploma in Engineering & Technology Programs 161

6.1: Accreditation Criteria for Diploma in Engg & Technology 161

6.2: Levels of Learning Outcomes for Diploma in Engineering & Technology Programs............................ 163

6.3: Tips to Respond to Typical Portions of the SAR Except Accreditation Criteria. 166

6.4: Tips for Preparing Typical Record Files Related to Institute and Program 167

7 NBA Accreditation of PG Technical Programs 179

7.1: Tips for Creating A SAR for ME & M Tech Programs............... 179

7.2: Tips for Creating A SAR For MCA Program.......................... 183

7.3: Tips for Creating A SAR For MBA Program For T-II Institutions 185

8 Quality Assurance Accreditation of Institutions by NAAC........... 189

8:1 Rationale... 189

8.2: NAAC Accreditation Approach 191

8.3: NAAC Accreditation Criteria...................................... 194

9 IAO Accreditation... 199

9.1 About IAO... 199

9.2: Benefits of IAO Accreditation 200

9.3: IAO'S Accreditation Process....................................... 201

9.4: IAO'S Accreditation Criteria 203

10 Selected References for Further Study 207

Illustrations

A: TABLES & PAGE NUMBER

T-1.1: Growth in AICTE Approved Intake of students
in Technical Institutions 23

T-4.1: Curriculum Analysis-1: BE Electronic &
Communications RGPV, Bhopal, MP, India 101

T-4.2: Curriculum Analysis-2: Model syllabi of Electronics and
communications (AICTE version-Oct., 2012)............................104

T-4.3: Example Specific Rubric or Rating scale 108

T-4.4: Specific Rubric or Check-list for Lab work:
Attainment of investigative & communication abilities...........109

T-4.5: GENERIC Tabular Rubric or Rating Scale 110

B: DIAGRAMS

Fig. 2.1: Ideal Technical Education System 37

Fig. 2.2: Relationship between vision,
Mission & values and PEOs & POs... 64

Fig. 3.1: The total process of aligning the assessment system.................... 90

Fig. 5.1: Pre-requisite Courses Chart 142

Fig. 5.2: Curriculum Development Model 144

CHAPTER: 1.0

ECONOMY AND TECHNICAL EDUCATION

1.1. Trends in & Status of Technical Education in India
1.2. Quality Assurance, Accreditation & economy
1.3. International Quality Assurance Accords
1.4. Regulation of Quality Assurance

1.1: TRENDS IN & STATUS OF TECHNICAL EDUCATION IN INDIA

India represents an emerging economies of the developing countries. India's **economy** is the **tenth-largest** in the world by nominal GDP and the **third-largest** by purchasing power parity (PPP). The Technical Education System (TES) of India is still being managed on the bases of guidelines established during a 200 years long British rule which was primarily meant to develop clerical subordinates to serve the British Rulers in ruling without any resentments and desire for innovations. The TES has been accommodating some innovations on the bases of indigenous & imported ideas from the fraternity of the world and the current system can be claimed to be more effective and was functioning fairly successfully till the last century.

During the first decade of the 21st century the world economy had been undergoing very fast changes and was passing through the cycles of recession and recovery, the earlier TES systems could not face the challenges of a dynamically changing environment due to continuous economic, social and cultural turmoil and the failures are being indicated in form of large number of engineers and similar professionals are wandering in the country without suitable jobs and without any courage to start their own enterprises. These unemployed talented youth can create a lot of social dissatisfaction and unrest amongst the young citizens and can halt the progress of the country, if quality of TES and other professional educational system do not follow the basic principles of Quality Assurance, in their educational enterprises which develops both the professional as well as employability skills and attitudes.

21st century seems to be in the era when a very ancient Indian Concept of "VASUDHEV KUTUMBKUM" (whole world is one family) is seen manifesting in several ways. Education in general and Technical Education in particular cannot remain unaffected entity. The graduates from technical institutions wish to serve the country as well as aspire to travel to other countries for undertaking further education & pursuing jobs and business, interacting with people, choosing a life partner and so on. To encourage such trans-country mobility of graduates makes it compulsory that the educational qualifications awarded in any one country ensures the following;

- Graduates become employable and ready to absorb soon in the industry or business without requiring long term orientation / training either in the country of origin or any other collaborating country.
- Graduate should pursue outcome based education which should ensure in them personality attributes which are comparable and compatible to the standardized graduate attributes globally accepted.
- Graduates of one country can pursue either employment or further studies in any other collaborating country without any need for establishing the equivalence between the degrees awarded by two different collaborating countries.

Washington, Sydney and Dublin accords were the result of fulfilling the above mentioned global requirements and we shall discuss more about Washington Accord in the later section of the chapter.

A representative Status of Technical Education in India:

To understand the trends in & current status of Technical Education System in the third world of developing countries the study of some typical features of trends in Indian Technical Education should be enough. Some of the facts described below has been formulated on the bases of information available on the website of All India Council of Technical Education (AICTE: http://www.aicte-india.org)

T-1.1: Growth in AICTE Approved Intake of students in Technical Institutions

Region	# of States	Growth in AICTE approved intake in all Dip/UG/PG in academic year				
		2008-09	2009-10	2010-11	2011-12	2012-13
Central	3	174,964	236,581	292,695	330,593	355,199
Eastern	11	103986	137929	168904	184648	194,283
North West	7	243754	308462	421740	476796	499,127
North-ern	3	157962	217197	304867	352575	392,997
South Central	1	316169	429819	536992	614671	691,237
South West	2	201761	242785	284606	316217	331,869
Suth-ern	2	294561	367282	432737	489112	542,844
West-ern	4	207168	260865	348194	399519	441,799
Grand Total	33	**1,700,325**	**2,200,920**	**2,790,735**	**3,164,131**	3,449,355
Growth wrt 2008		100%	129.44%	129.92%	186.09%	**202.86%**

B: *Growth in number of Institutions in India from 2006-07 to 2012-13*

- Engineering = 3498/1511= 2,31 or 231%
- All programs Engg & Management, Pharmacy, Hotel management & catering Technology, Master of Computer Applications, Architecture = 8598/4491 = 1.91 or 191%

C: Growth in # of AICTE approved Intake of students in 'branch-wise' format during period from 2006-07 to 2012-13

- Engineering = 176976/550986 = 3.2 or 320%,
- Management = 385008/94704 = 4.06 or 406%
- MCA = 100700/56805 = 1.77 or 177%
- Pharmacy = 121652/39517 = 3.08 or 308%
- Architecture = 5996/4543 = 1.31 or 131%

D: Growth in number of NBA accredited programs (Dip/UG/PG) in Technical Colleges in India during the year

- During 2006-7 about 6 to 7%
- During 2012-13 about 10 to 12 %
- During 2013-14 about 3 to 4 %

Unfortunately, a very dangerous trend is emerging that in campus and off campus placements of graduates is not growing in proportions of the intake of students in the professional institutions which is the indication of the bad status of quality assurance of technical and other professional educational services in India and in other developing countries in ASIA and elsewhere. If not improved this can lead to a great socio-political unrest in the developing countries.

M/s EdCIL (India) Limited is a Government of India Enterprise which provides admission services of foreign nationals and NRIs in only those institutions which offer accredited programs by the regulatory bodies like NBA, NAAC and MCI etc. The professional Institutions in developing countries ignore the importance of Quality Assurance of their services which very much obvious in the information furnished above.

It is strange & frustrating to observe that in an emerging and potentially world leading economy like India, the number of accredited programs are lowering after National Board of Accreditation or NBA, Ministry of HRD, India introduced *'Outcome based Accreditation System'* in Jan 2013. The author also experienced the same trend in practice while doing his consultancy work for providing assistance for NBA/ NAAC/ IAO accreditation of programs & the Institutions. Some of the institutions who initiated efforts for accreditation, dropped the idea for applying for accreditation due to the complexity of the newly introduced outcome based accreditation system. This is the reason for writing this book which in my opinion should be removing or reducing some of many doubts in the minds of managers and faculty of the institutions.

Despite the desire many institutions got discouraged due to lack of specific information to facilitate the process of filling the self-assessment Report (SAR) for applying for accreditation, which also require;

- Substantial investments in acquiring enhanced physical and better human resources to justify the eligibility,
- Creating of large number of files as evidences to statements made in the SAR (for NBA)/ Self-Study Report (SSP for NAAC & IAO.) for getting the acceptance of the accreditation agency.

Govt. of India had launched a Technical Education Quality Improvement Program (TEQIP) in 2004 after taking heavy loan from the World Bank. Its Project Implementation Plan document (PIP-2009) gives the following scenario of Indian Technical Education.

- The exponential growth in Technical Education has, however, not translated into any significant growth in the number of quality Graduates due to restricted availability of qualified faculty. There is currently a wide gap between quality and quantity in Technical Education.
- The quality of education and training being imparted in the Engineering Education institutions varies from excellent to poor, with some institutions comparing favorably with the best in the world and others suffering from different degrees of handicaps. There is a gap between the educational standards of the Indian Institutes of Technology (IITs) and other Engineering institutions. The few IITs can neither change the fate of the whole country nor improve the entire Educational System.
- Concerted efforts are required to bridge the gap in the quality of education between IITs and other institutions. The IITs have to act as a catalyst in the growth of quality Technical Education in the country,

and play a major role in training faculty from the other institutions of the India in both teaching and research.

- At present, Industry- Institutes collaboration is at a nascent stage. Industry-Academia collaboration involves two key aspects—inputs to curriculum development and internships for students. Increasing Industry-Academia collaboration requires: (i) overcoming the distrust between the two partners; (ii) identification of win-win partnerships in terms of sharing technical knowledge; and (iii) incentives to institutions and faculty for collaboration.

- Obsolete learning infrastructure prevents the development of hands-on skills in Industry-relevant technologies. Many institutions have not upgraded their equipment, laboratories, and learning resources for even more than a decade. There is also the absence of curriculum revisions that focus on practical training and quality instructions, research and development.

- Encouraging Stagnating research that caters to the emergent Industry and societal demand for technological solutions results in directly and indirectly improving knowledge and quality of faculty, which in turn would benefit students. A growing number of Indian firms are keen to collaborate with academia to enhance their competitiveness. Active research programs in engineering institutions would also make meaningful contribution for sustainable technological development in India.

The goal of TEQIP program gives the best description of the status of Technical Education in Developing Countries

To scale-up and support ongoing efforts of the Government of India to improve quality of Technical Education and enhance existing capacities of the institutions to become dynamic, demand-driven, quality conscious, efficient and forward looking, responsive to rapid economic and technological developments occurring at the local, State, National and International levels. It has a clear focus on the objectives to improve the overall quality of existing Engineering Education.

1.2: ECONOMY, QUALITY ASSURANCE AND ACCREDITATION

An **economy** or **economic system** consists of the production, distribution or trade, and consumption of limited goods and services by different agents in a given geographical location. The economic agents can be individuals, businesses, organizations, or governments. Transactions occur when two parties agree to the value or price of the transacted good or service, commonly expressed in a certain currency. A given economy is the result of a set of processes that involves its culture, values, education, technological evolution, history, social organization, political structure and legal systems, as well as its geography, natural resource endowment, and ecology, as main factors. These factors give context, content, and set the conditions and parameters in which an economy functions.

A market-based economy is where goods and services are produced without obstruction or interference, and exchanged according to demand and supply between participants (economic agents) by barter or a medium of exchange or currency. Market based economies require transparency on information, such as true prices, to work, and may include various kinds of immaterial production, such as affective labor that describes work carried out that is intended to produce or modify emotional experiences in people, but does not have a tangible, physical product as a result. Therefore Outcome based professional education system synchronizes with the market based economy where the outcome in terms of learning outcomes are specifies and accomplished commensurate with what was assured at the time of admission of a student.

Educational enterprises provide services which had been classified as Business Enterprise by WTO in Jan 2005. WTO feels the need of more commitment and settlement of issues related to clarity of rules of admission /tuition fee, transparency in outcomes, facilitation of cross border mobility of student-customers, and transferability of credits of prior learning in one country to other etc. Slowly education has been recognized as a major agent influencing the rate of growth of economy of an area or a country.

Professional Education is an important factor directly influencing the economy, which is responsible for providing services related to education, training and R&D needed to produce new products or services from natural resources and their subsequent by-products. Technical Education is most directly related to market driven economy as it is responsible to educate &

train and ensure that passing out graduates are prepared to serve in positions in industry and commerce to contribute directly and indirectly in making industry economically not only viable but profitable.

The human values of professionals produced by the so called modern institutions and universities, in opinion of the author are dwindling because of the fact that the democracies were adopted by such countries which were supposed to be secular in its operations which unfortunately was interpreted by commercial minded owner of the higher education as well as many politicians that there should not be any good or bad influence of religion on the education system of a big country like India. Thus the educated graduates coming out of such religion neutral institutions do not have good human values. The result of such a situation is manifesting in terms of graduates' dis-respect to elders and hard work, lack of integrity, corrupt practices to earn faster, limited sensitivity towards interests of other people of communities and countries at large, shattering families, ever increasing cases of divorce, stressful lifestyles and feeling of loneliness in crowd of coworkers.

Quality Assurance: Quality as a concept can be defined as any product or process which is; 1. **Fit for Purpose, & 2. Right at the first time.** This Product or Service must meet the requirements of the customer and either create customer satisfaction or possibly delight. If anything is fit for a purpose and it must meet specifications & purpose which is right at the first time.

Quality Assurance (QA) is a way of preventing occurrence of mistakes or defects in manufactured products and avoiding problems when delivering services to customers possibly for the first time.

For instance, in case of delivery of higher educational services, the purpose is to transform the raw school graduate student into an educated professional person having knowledge & skills relevant to selected area of work and enable him/her to perform functions right for the first time for family, for community, for country and for the globe. Unfortunately, many educationists carry a wrong concept that the purpose of institutions & education is to enable students to pass University examinations with higher grade or higher percentage of marks only and they do not take adequate care to make him/her an employable, committed & competent citizen of the country and the globe.

Earlier Technical Education and Training used to be delivered by Govt. and Govt. aided institutions and the tuition fee was quite less because the Govt. used to bear the major expenditure of operating the services. Govt. used to think education was an essential social service. With the growth of economy, the living standards improved, paying capacity of people was enhanced and proportionately the tuition fee kept on increasing with time. At this juncture somewhere in early 1990's private organizations started investing in establishing new professional institutions and universities. After this period professional education was no longer remained a charitable social service. Private Institutions became business entities and profit centers and self-financing enterprises.

The recent current measures of quality of technical education system were based on older criteria related inputs and processes plus to some extent on quality of outputs. Nobody seem to bother about quality of the program outcomes. Program Outcomes (POs) are those multiple effects on students which are acquired during years of program study and are directly related to the technical competence as well as personality traits/employability skills of the graduates.

The accreditation process is the certification process of the quality and quantity of implementation of quality assurance in an educational enterprise. The earlier model (in & before 2012) of NBA Accreditation System was based on the input, process and to some extent outputs. Countries like India which has very young population (around 35 years), cannot sustain its economic growth with deficient personality traits and employability skills in its young professional graduates and work-force. Perhaps, Because of this dependence of the economy on professional education, Govt. of India and Governments of surrounding countries thought it desirable to get membership in various International Accords like Washington Accord (in 1987) and Sydney and Dublin accords (after 2000).

The new quality assurance and accreditation system in India and surrounding countries like Srilanka, Pakistan and Bangladesh has been adopted upon the recommendations of Washington Accord which operates on the outcome based technical education system. Outcome based system is in vogue in the Technical Institutions in USA & other western countries since last two decades or more.

During the last decade the investment of Private Entrepreneurs in Technical & Professional education has increased multifold. Payment of much higher matching tuition fee has become the issue of economic viability of the educational enterprises. Population has seen steep growth of economy and income of people, and family leader's aspirations, business profits, the scope and reach of an educational enterprise. Economically the world has become a small village. It is natural that the educational Institutions would like to admit students from all other states of the country as well as foreign countries to make the institutions more viable and sustainable.

The expansion of private educational enterprises from one country to the whole world has many legal, social, cultural and economic implications. The most important implication is to establish equivalence of degrees so that the qualifications awarded by the University of one Country can be accepted by other country for admissions in further education programs and undertake jobs and render independent consultancy services. This situation has been highlighted very aptly in the UNESCO Report given below:

Quality assurance and accreditation (<u>UNESCO report 2002</u>)

a. *Increased cross border education delivery and a set of legal rules and obligations in trade agreements require that urgent attention be given to the question of quality assurance and accreditation of **education providers**.*

b. *Not only is it important to have **national mechanisms** which have the capacity to address accreditation and quality assessment procedures for the academic programs of new private and foreign providers, it is equally important that attention be given to developing an **international approach to quality assurance and accreditation**.*

c. *There is growing awareness that in the world of cross border **education trade**, **national quality assurance schemes are becoming challenged** by the complexities of the international education environment. While there may be growing awareness, there is no acceptance or agreement that harmonization of national policies with an international approach to quality assessment and accreditation is needed.*

d. *It is imperative that* **education specialists discuss and determine the appropriate regulating mechanisms** *at the national and international level and not leave these questions to the designers and arbitrators of trade agreements.*

e. *Another, potentially contentious issue is the* **application of quality assurance schemes to both domestic and foreign providers***. It may well be that under certain conditions, the national treatment obligation requires that all providers, domestic and foreign, be subject to the same processes and criteria.*

,,

1.3: INTERNATIONAL QUALITY ASSURANCE ACCORDS

Under the pressure of WTO and the compulsion of facilitating smooth mobility of Professionals educated in Indian Technical Institutions, MHRD, Govt of India applied and got provisional membership of Washington Accord (1987), that is, in the first decade of 21st century, along with four other countries namely; Germany, Bangladesh, Pakistan and Srilanka.

In all three agreements operate at globally recognized levels of professional qualification, and provide the mechanism for mutual recognition between signatory bodies of:

- **Washington Accord** (1987) - engineering education accreditation processes at Chartered /Professional Engineer level. (12+4 Years Degree programs)
- **Sydney Accord** (2001)- engineering education accreditation processes at Incorporated Engineer/Engineering Technologist level (10+ 3 years diploma programs)
- **Dublin Accord (2002)** - qualifications which underpin the granting of Engineering Technician titles (10+2 years Certificate programs)

The **Washington Accord**, signed among six countries in 1989, is an International Agreement among bodies responsible for accrediting under graduate engineering degree programs. It recognizes the substantial equivalency of programs accredited by those bodies and recommends that graduates of programs accredited by any of the signatory bodies be recognized by the other bodies as having met the academic requirements for entry to the practice of engineering in the area of their jurisdiction.

India represented by the National Board of Accreditation, MHRD, New-Delhi was accepted as a provisional member of the **Washington Accord** in the year **2007** and is still holding the provisional member status. By conferring provisional status, the signatories have indicated their confidence that NBA-AICTE has the potential capability to reach full signatory status. NBA is preparing to apply for permanent signatory status of Washington Accord under the guidance of the mentors appointed by IEA Secretariat (Secretariat of Washington Accord). The new **outcome based system of accreditation of Engg programs** has been developed over a period from Jan 2009 till Dec 2012. The documents facilitating preparing **Self-assessment report (SAR)** by the interested institution or Department had been finalized by **Jan 31, 2012**. NBA has started conducting accreditation visits since **Jan 2013**. NBA's outcome based Accreditation Documents had been finalized so far cover programs in Engg & Technology (Dip, UG & PG), Pharmacy (Dip, UG & PG), MBA, MCA, Hospitality Management (UG), and Tourism Management (PG).

Each member organization has expressed its confidence in the quality assurance processes of the others. This leads to mutual recognition of accredited engineering qualifications and, generally, to exemption from the education requirement for practice in each of the signatory countries. The detailed documents of agreements are available on the website of International Engg Alliance (www.ieagreements.org).

Sydney Accord (2001; equivalence of 10+ 3 years diploma or technologist programs): It is an agreement between the bodies responsible for accrediting professional engineering technologist programs in each of the signatory countries. It recognizes the substantial equivalency of programs accredited by those bodies, and recommends that graduates of accredited programs in any of the signatory countries be recognized by the other countries as having met the academic requirements for entry to the practice of engineering. The Sydney Accord covers Engineering technology. There are 9 full signatory members of the accord. One member has provisional signatory status. Some clues are existing implying that India is also preparing to apply for acquiring first provisional membership in this accord. However, the documents facilitating Polytechnic Colleges of India have been prepared for acquiring NBA Accreditation of

Dip in Engg programs. These documents are available on the website of NBA (www.nbaind.org).

Dublin Accord (2002, 10+2 years Certificate or engineering technician programs)**:** It is an agreement between the bodies responsible for accrediting engineering technician programs in each of the signatory countries. It recognizes the substantial equivalency of programs accredited by those bodies, and recommends that graduates of accredited programs in any of the signatory countries be recognized by the other countries as having met the academic requirements for entry to the practice of engineering. Presently there are 8 full signatory members of this accord. Other countries may join it in near future.

1.4: REGULATION OF QUALITY ASSURANCE

National Board of Accreditation or NBA is the regulating authority for evaluation and certification of quality assurance of Engg/ Technology programs in India. NBA represents India in Washington Accord group. In the same way every signatory country has a regulating body which regulates and certifies QA Accreditation. The following list indicates the regulating bodies of all the signatory countries of Washington Accord.

Full signatory members of Washington Accord (www.nbaind.org)

- **Australia** - Represented by Engineers Australia (*1989*)
- **Canada** - Represented by Engineers Canada (*1989*)
- **Chinese Taipei** - Represented by Institute of Engineering Education Taiwan (*2007*)
- **Hong Kong China** - Represented by The Hong Kong Institution of Engineers (*1995*)
- ***India***: represented by National board of Technical Education (www.nbaind.org), (June 2014)
- **Ireland** - Represented by Engineers Ireland (1989)
- **Japan** - Represented by Japan Accreditation Board for Engineering Education (2005)

- **Korea** - Represented by Accreditation Board for Engineering Education of Korea (2007)
- **Malaysia** - Represented by Board of Engineers Malaysia (2009)
- **New Zealand** - Represented by Institution of Professional Engineers NZ (1989)
- **Russia** - Represented by Association for Engineering Education of Russia (2012)
- **Singapore** - Represented by Institution of Engineers Singapore (2006)
- **South Africa** - Represented by Engineering Council of South Africa (1999)
- ***Sri Lanka** - Represented by Institution of Engineers Sri Lanka (June 2014)
- **Turkey** - Represented by MUDEK (2011)
- **United Kingdom** - Represented by Engineering Council UK (1989)
- **United States** - Represented by Accreditation Board for Engineering and Technology (1989)

*Please note that **India and Sri Lanka** have become full signatory members recently on 13th **June 2014** (Ref: International Engineering Alliance)*

Provisional Members

- **Bangladesh** - represented by Board of Accreditation for Engineers for Engineering and Technical Education
- **China** - represented by China Association for Science and Technology Pakistan Engineering Council
- **Pakistan** - represented by Pakistan Engineering Council
- **Peru** - represented by ICACIT
- **Philippines** - represented by Philippine Technological Council (Ref: International Engineering Alliance)

CHAPTER 2.0

OUTCOME BASED TECHNICAL EDUCATION

2.1. Current Technical Education System in India

2.2. Outcome based Technical Education (OBET)

2.3. Performing SWOT Analysis of the Department and the institute

2.4. Evolving Shared Vision, Mission & Values

2.5. Program Educational objectives (PEOs)

2.6. Program (Learning) Outcomes (POs)

2.1: CURRENT TECHNICAL EDUCATION SYSTEM IN INDIA

The system: The current unaccredited technical education programs & systems are giving more emphases on the inputs and processes related to managing, administration, teaching & learning, a fraction of output in the form of results of University examinations and a partial outcome as award of graduation degree by the university. Nobody so far seems to be thinking in terms of outcomes, manifesting in technical competence along with employability skills, what to say about implementation of outcome based technical education. Let us try to understand some of the implications of the constituent elements of the system.

1. **Input**: It includes human resources such as students admitted for transformation, syllabi, university rules, faculty and all other staff, managers & Governors of the Institute and physical resources. The physical resources include land and buildings, laboratories & workshop and other infrastructure items like roads, parks, hostels, canteen & mess complex etc. Financial resources shall include accounting records, financial inputs and working capital etc. Administrative inputs like rules, regulations and records of resources. It may also include all the instructions and mandatory bindings of the affiliating University and Regulating agencies like AICTE, DTE & NBA etc.

2. **Processes:** The primary processes in an educational institute is group of academic (related to direct interactions between teacher and taught) or teaching and learning processes such a set of teaching methods of different learning spaces- classroom, laboratories, workshops and project work etc. Learning processes are generally taken care by providing learning resources such as Library of books, magazines, journals, on-line resources and digital material on CDs, pen-drives and other storage devices/ appliances. Secondary learning processes are co-curricular assignments & preparations related to the terminal evaluation of students by internal and external assessment instruments. Tertiary learning processes shall include all processes which help in indirect processes of learning through extracurricular activities and taking care of general health and well-being of the students and other residents of the campus.

3. **Outputs:** the outputs include results of internal and external examinations, experience in teachers and students, appreciation from the parents, employers & other stake holders.

4. **Feedback:** When the institute monitors continuously the performance of each student, Department and institute as a whole, the mechanisms of feedback are installed to monitor the performance of individual faculty and staff, Director and Head of the Departments and even the senior managers / governors of the institute. The evaluative feedback is taken by comparing with the actual achievements of a group of pre-declared targets within a given time frame.

5. **Outcomes:** Outcome is a consolidated learning impact on a graduate which were experienced during all interactions inside & outside the traditional learning spaces, on every working day of four years of the Engg Degree program. Most of the faculty and managers of technical education seldom think of outcome of all the curricular, co-curricular and extra-curricular activities which students

go through the program duration. It is something like many painters painting on a big canvas without thinking why they are painting and ultimately what shall come out as a resulting painting on the canvas.

Feed-forward: Feed-forward is a phenomenon of learning lessons from past mistakes and experiences. After proper evaluation, if the Board of Governors (BoG) of the Institute identifies certain mistakes, experiences and inferences, which should be considered during the planning & implementation of reforms in the subsequent year, shall fall in the category of feed-forward. This clearly implies that the institute has installed continuous quality improvement mechanisms from whereby the data on performance are constantly collected, analyzed, policies are reviewed and inferences drawn for feeding-forward to process subsequent batch.

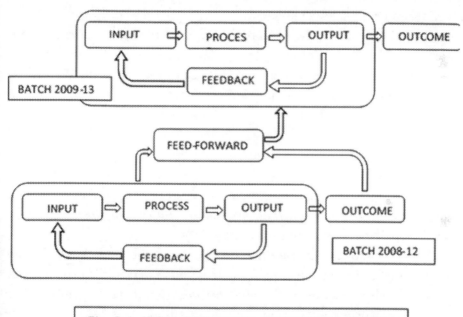

Fig. 2.1: IDEAL TECHNICAL EDUCATION SYSTEM

- Yearly lessons can be learned from the deviations of outputs from its target values.
- In case of BE Engg programs, most important lessons can be learned at the end of four years when the deviations of outcomes from its target values are analyzed.

The **ideal Technical Education System** has been displayed in the figure 2.1. The current TE system does not consider the subsystems of outcome and feed-forward. This relationship has been displayed in such a way that the feed-forward can be given every four years across the subsequent batches on the bases of the outcomes. However, it is also possible to feed-forward at the end of every semester on the bases of the experiences in implementing innovative educational reforms in the sub-systems of inputs and processes. Thus the quality assurance is a continuous journey and not the destination as some people wrongly understand so.

Current technical education system: The **Outcome** and **Feed-forward** are two concepts which are generally ignored the current course based input to output model of the Technical Education System in most developing countries as the current Technical Education System mostly takes care of inputs and processes and outputs to some extent.

The major hurdle to change is policy input in the format of curriculum which is decided by the university to which an institute is affiliated as well as all the conditions of the outputs are also defined by the university. Most of the Private or self-financing technical institutes do not have any say in designing and developing both curricula and the examination system of the university. This hurdle discourages innovations in the modifications & implementation of curriculum and its students' performance assessment. The current curriculum design is based upon the traditional teaching of more theory courses rather than imparting skills of applying engineering theory which make graduates more *ready to work in industrial or commercial environment* and make graduates, problem solvers for the industry / commerce.

In case of subject based curriculum teaching, the stress is on scoring marks or grades in individual courses. It becomes very difficult to predict specifically, what traits of professional personality will be acquired by the graduates immediately after graduation. This traditional insensitivity towards professional Personality traits or soft skills in the graduates seems to be the biggest cause of making outcome based system incomprehensible and *which has ultimately retarded the rate of growth of accredited programs during last few years.*

It is hoped that the new outcome based **NBA Accreditation System** shall promote Curriculum Development on the basis of (LEARNING) **OUTCOMES** rather than focusing on (teaching of) THEORY **SUBJECTS**.

In terms of NBA the current system of technical education follows INPUT-OUTPUT MODEL.

2.2: OUTCOME BASED TECHNICAL EDUCATION SYSTEM (OBTE):

Important concepts: Since, the need of understanding outcome based technical education system arises out of the desire to understand the complexities of outcome based accreditation system so it is better to define a few concepts related to accreditation of Quality Assurance. We should prefer to assume that every educational entrepreneur (Owner) owning the Technical Institute would like to run the enterprise efficiently and effectively and earn some reasonable profit as well. They only need to realize that delivery of quality educational service is vital for faster economic growth of all stake holders; graduates, their family, owners of institutes, concerned Governments, country and the world as a whole.

Primary Outcome: In OBTE, the impact of four years' of interactive experiences of engineering graduates are defined and highly focused and they are expressed in terms of Graduate Attributes: the personality traits a professional Engineer and its desirable employability skills. It is aimed at making graduates responsible, competent and employable professionals who shall contribute towards the economy, profession & people in a balanced way. Being a good professional Engineer is necessary but not sufficient; the professional engineer is ought to be a good human who is sensitive to other human beings' and communities' quality of life as well.

Secondary outcomes include more responsible, sensitive committed and creative faculty & staff.

Tertiary Outcome is enhanced brand-value of the institute which helps in attracting both talented faculty as well as better learners (students) who shall come out as better performing scholars and competent engineers.

- **Accreditation**: It is a formal recognition & certification of quality delivery of technical education program offered by an institute by authorized regulating agency. In case of India, AICTE should have approved the institute and programs. NBA shall certify for accreditation after two batches have successfully graduated from the program.

- **Paradigm shift in Assessment parameters for accreditation system**:

    o **For Input output based assessment-** Infrastructure, Students, Faculty, Support Staff, Management, Curriculum, Calendar, pass %, Number of publications, placements etc.

    o **For Outcome based assessment-** What knowledge, skill and behavior a graduate is expected to attain upon just completion of program, and after 3 to 4 years of graduation, Observable / and Measurable abilities or outcomes. Graduate Attributes (GA) defined by NBA or Washington Accord, This necessitates mapping of outcomes with GA, Objectives, Mission and Vision

- **POs: Program outcomes:** POs are expressed in terms of knowledge, skills and behaviors learned or acquired by the students at the time of graduation. They are aligned and synchronized with Global or NBA's Graduate Attributes. POs are the statements which facilitate & ensure global mobility of graduates in the signatory countries of Accords like Washington Accord.

- **PEOs: Program Educational Objectives:** PEOs are broad statements describe the career and professional accomplishments that the program is preparing the graduate to achieve. It indicates the potential fields of employment & professional accomplishments of the graduate within 3-4 years after graduation. These are the statements made by the Academic Department of the institute which offer the educational program like BE or B Tech. These statements are derived from the vision, mission, goals and priority. All these concepts can be formulated when one performs SWOT analyses on the Institute and the concerned departments

- **SWOT: S**trengths, **W**eaknesses, pertaining to the concerned Institute, Department and Faculty and **O**pportunities & **T**hreats outside the institute and departments offering the program. This analyses helps in fixing priorities of actions by the department and the institute based on their strengths and take other actions after overcoming to a great extent the weaknesses of the Department / institute.

- **Vision** is the better image and status of your institute in future you desire to develop, described in present tense, as if it were happening now. It is where you aspire to reach and be like. In other words, Vision is a futuristic statement that the department / institution aspire to achieve after a selected time frame. For BE programs the period of future should be of order of 8 to 10 years.

- **Mission** elaborates reason why institute exists and wants to excel further through a variety of ways & means so as to reach the vision as soon as possible or at least in the targeted time period. Usually the mission statements are **means** & expressions of approaches to achieve the vision.

- **COs or Course Outcomes:** these are clear statements of what a student should be able to demonstrate upon completion of learning a course.

- **Course:** a set of organized knowledge, skill & attitudes to be learned under an approved subject title. A course may be a theory subject, or experiential learning through a lab or project work or industrial or field training

- **Modules:** a group of allied courses to be learnt/ taught to achieve MOs, POs & PEOs. As per AICTE's Model Curriculum of (B.E.) program (www.aicte-india.org) the following are the course clusters or Modules for a 4 year BE or B Tech program

    - o   **HS** – Humanities and Social Sciences Courses
    - o   **BS** – Basic Science Courses
    - o   **ES** – Engineering Sciences Courses
    - o   **PC** – Professional Core Courses
    - o   **PE** – Professional Electives Courses
    - o   **OE** – Open Electives Courses
    - o   **PT** – Project work and Training in industry or field
    - o   **MC** – Mandatory Courses

Assessment: There are different types of assessments;

- **Continuous Assessment-** It takes place during the progress of learning process. This assessment needs to be undertaken continuously and its purpose is to ensure that the earlier items have been learnt before proceeding to next item. It is also known as **Formative Assessment**.
- **Terminal Assessment-** It takes place at the end of a term of learning-teaching session. It is undertaken for grading the learners as per their learning achievements expressed in terms of grades or marks. It is also known as **Summative Assessment**.
- **Assessment Rubrics:** Rubric is an organized **set of performance indicators** which define and describe the **important components of a technical task** being completed in line with the instructions of an assignment. The rubrics may relate to assessment of a generic task or a specific task. Rubrics in general, are desirable in order to improve objectivity of assessment where the qualitative measures are unavoidable in assessment.

Let us compare the existing and outcome based technical education systems.

Input-output based system starts with the cluster of courses which should be taught and the syllabi describes the organization of constituent courses, their contents & schemes of terminal examinations and sessional work, over the years of programs. Here the focus is only to secure good grade or marks in examination of individual theoretical courses and some practical work whose purpose is neither clearly understood and nor clearly explained in the syllabi documents. Over a period of time unfortunately all the activities slowly get aligned towards passing the examinations with good grades/ marks and teachers simply start forgetting why are they teaching a specific course? Most faculty fail to understand the connections between a course with both the profession as well as the how the course shall be applied to the world of work.

Outcome based system starts with identifying the abilities (POs) required by the world of work and POs alignment with global Graduate Attributes (GAs) which shall ensure global mobility of graduates. The department writes Program's Educational Objectives or PEOs, in view of SWOT analyses. Then

Curriculum is developed to accomplish both PEOs and POs, with elaborate description to ensure effective delivery of elements of education and training during each semester without forgetting the need of doing assessment of performance of each student within the relevant curricular, co-curricular and extra-curricular activities through their continuous & terminal assessment methods and instruments.

Quality Assurance ensures that learning and practice of intended abilities are accomplished. The following three logical steps defines the Outcome Based Education System

1. **Curriculum documentation** is focused on defining and accomplishing the Program Outcomes (POs) in alignment with Graduate Attributes, immediately at the time of graduation.
2. Keeping records of direct and indirect assessment during all the eight/ six semesters, collating and compiling all the records of assessment of each individual student in order to certifying at the time of graduation, what POs the student had acquired.
3. Implementing the curriculum in such a way that the students achieve POs as well the department achieves PEOs of the Program for which the monitoring shall continue till 3 to 4 years after graduation of the batch admitted after accreditation.

Outcome based system also attempts to solve another global problem of facilitating the mobility of graduates from one country to another country. Washington Accord has provided a pragmatic solution to the problem of mobility by standardizing the Global Graduate Attributes which provide a bench mark while writing down the POs.

Let us also try to understand the requirement of Washington Accord in this context.

Requirements of Washington accord: The Washington Accord signed original by 6 full signatory countries in 1987 laid down the broader policies of the accord and Graduate Attributes. The purpose of the accord was to mutually recognize and accept the qualifications accredited by signatories. Presently there are 17 full signatories including India and 5 provisional signatories including China & Pakistan. The requirements of the accord in brief are;

➤ Members of accord must follow Outcome based (Technical) education system.

➤ All the members must accept the **standardized Graduate Attributes** (GAs) for their graduates to accomplish. It is because of this requirements the POs are aligned with GAs.

➤ If any provisional member wants to reap the benefits of its large human resources and to become a knowledge society and global supplier of trained human resources, it must become a full signatory member. Thus, after acquiring full signatory member status India needs to implement the outcome based accreditation system in the Engineering Colleges meticulously, robustly and honestly. India and Sri Lanka got full signatory status during June 2014 and both can learn from each other by sharing experiences and expertise on innovations practiced to implement Outcome based technical education services in with professional commitment to improve their own complex economies.

Adopt OBTE: NBA, MHRD, Govt. of India has now become full member of Washington accord, and therefore Indian Technical Institutions must take its benefits at an earlier date in acquiring global recognition through NBA Accreditation. To facilitate the faster achievement, the Indian Technical Institutions and Technical Universities should adopt Outcome based Technical Education System which shall facilitate both mobility of technical graduates world over as well attract foreign students to the Technical Institutions of India. Such a situation surely shall result into better profitability and sustainability of accredited institutes as well as it shall contribute positively to boost India's economy. This statement is applicable to any other country desirous in embracing the OBTE.

The following pages describe a few important steps which should be understood for smooth transition from the current Input- Output based Technical Education System to OBTE.

- Performing SWOT Analysis
- Evolving Shared Vision, Missions and Values
- Formulating Program Educational Objectives
- Developing Program Outcomes

2.3: PERFORMING SWOT ANALYSIS OF
THE DEPARTMENT AND THE INSTITUTE

SWOT is an acronym of four words: *STRENGTH, WEAKNESS, OPPORTUNITIES and THREATS*. SWOT, is an analytical method, which is used in strategic planning of the operations of the institutions. Strategic planning is a process in which future aims are determined together with the stakeholders and responsibilities & sources are allocated in accordance with these future aims. It is a process of planning the movement of institute from the current status point to a targeted status point as implied the goals of planned growth of the institute over a certain planned period of time. The concept of strategic planning is closely related with the concept of foresight, which is in simple words, the collection of systematic efforts of managers for attaining the best possible choice of specified future.

SWOT is a first stage of planning which helps to focus on key issues. The role of SWOT analysis is to take the information from the environmental scan and separate it into internal and external issues. SWOT analysis determines if the information indicates something that will assist the institution in accomplishing its objectives. SWOT can be done for the total institution or for a single department.

Strengths: Perceptions for which you feel proud of and you wish to utilize to the maximum extent to further improve quality and productivity of your efforts. Ask yourselves? Questions such as: What do you do well? What unique resources can you draw on? & what do others see as your strengths? The Strengths can also be identified by thinking in terms of capabilities, recognition, competitive advantages, resources, assets, people (experience, knowledge, their culture, values, attitudes and behaviors), innovative aspects, marketing, quality of programs & curriculum, location, accreditations, qualifications, certifications, and processes/systems etc. Analysis should highlight which one to be exploited first and for what purpose to the best advantages of the institute.

Weaknesses: Feelings which at times prevent to perform at a higher level than what you are able to do at present, which you desire to remove as early as possible to improve level/ quality of your work. Helpful questions are: What could you improve? Where do you have fewer resources than others? & what are others likely to see as weaknesses? The Weaknesses can be identified by thinking in terms of disadvantages, gaps in capabilities; lack of competitive strength, reputation, financial, timescales/deadlines, weak core activities, distractions, morale, leadership, accreditations, continuity, robustness and processes/systems, more focus on Teaching & no concern to check for learning, Director spends more time in administration rather ensuring learning by students & faculty. Director has no time to look into what the teachers are doing behind the closed doors of the classrooms or labs. Whether or not students are learning? Whether or not students' feedback properly analyzed to ensure continuous improvements in the performance of faculty? Analysis should prioritize the subcomponents to be sorted out first to minimize the risks of failures and so on.

Opportunities: available in the environment which we must use to our advantage to attract more and talented students, educate and train our students to make them more capable engineers & so on. Ask questions like…What opportunities are open to you?, what trends could you take advantage of? & how can you turn your strengths into opportunities? The Opportunities can be identified by thinking in terms of market developments, competitor vulnerabilities, industry trends, and geographical partnerships, Technology development and innovation, Research in niche areas & Industry Institution partnership, conducting in-housing orientation / training of faculty & staff., and constituting self-learning groups of faculty, staff and students. Analysis should highlight which one to be exploited first and for what purpose in the best interests of the institute?

Threats: which are present around us and creating problems and hurdles for us to slow down or stop our fast progress to excel and our becoming the main target of students for quality Engg. Education what we can provide otherwise. Helpful questions can be: What threats could harm you?, what is your competition doing? & what threats do your weaknesses expose you to? The Threats can be identified by thinking in terms of external forces that could inhibit the maintenance or attainment of a competitive advantage or any unfavorable situation in the external or internal environment that is potentially damaging present and future, allurement of good faculty by a nearby Private College by paying slightly more salary / allowances etc., negative myth: Quality showmanship of faculty controls quality of learning by students. Analysis should prioritize the subcomponents to be sorted out first to minimize the risks of failures.

Steps in SWOT Analysis:

i. **Stake holder participation**- Identify the stakeholders of an Institution such as students, parents, faculty, managers and other staff, Regulators and Industry. Invite a representative sample persons belonging to each category. Using brain storming and other creativity methods explore the views & perceptions of the stake holders regarding Strength & Weakness as internal issues of the Institute/ Department, and Opportunities & threats as external issues.

ii. **Analysis 1**: You may also attempt to use written responses which take more compilation and analysis time. At the end about 10 to 12 major strengths & Weaknesses and 6 to 8 opportunities & Threats should be selected in the order of the frequency of the perceptions of the stakeholders.

iii. **Analysis 2:** Get the semi-final statements of SWOT validated with a mixed group of stakeholders and listen carefully what they comment and finalize the table of SWOT in consultation with them.

iv. **Analysis 3:** It is also possible to consider the combinations of Strength and Opportunities as well as Weaknesses and Threats to understand the best possible and worst possible situations in the life of the institute or Department. This kind of analysis shall give the range of variations of the situation which the manager has to use for undertaking strategic planning of Departments and the whole institute.

All the three analyses shall be helpful in evolving Vision & Mission of the Department and the whole institute. Such decisions fall in the class of informed decisions.

A set of sample SWOT statements are given just to provide an idea to faculty members those who would like to conduct SWOT analyses without the help of a management expert. However, in case of the Engg Colleges, they can always consult the Management School within their group of institutions.

Sample SWOT Statements for a typical Engg College in a developing country may be something similar to the following statements.

Sample Strengths:

S1 Well laid down vision & mission with supportive and cooperative Management.

S2 Spacious classrooms with audio visual facilities which can accommodate students comfortably

S3 Adequately big central library facilities

S4 Qualified, experienced and dedicated faculty.

S5 Motivating work culture and adequately positive environment

S6 Good & impressive Institute Buildings with adequate infrastructure

S7 Sufficient number of Laboratories with some testing facilities.

S8 Expert lectures are delivered by industrial & other professionals on regular basis.

S9 Generating Revenue by R&D consultancy projects.

S10 Well laid down processes & procedures for academics and administration.

S11 Consultancy & Entrepreneurship Dev Cell (CEDC) has become operational.

S12 Students' performance in university exams is satisfactory.

S13 Professional Students chapters are active.

S14 Many extra-curricular activities including NCC & NSS schemes

S15 Many co-curricular activities are undertaken by students under guidance of faculty & staff like: Tech-fest, Fine art, models & projects' exhibitions, rich cultural annual functions to ignite & nurture creativity.

Sample weaknesses:

W1. Emphasis on examination oriented teaching rather than students centric practice oriented learning-teaching.

W2. less number of & inadequately qualified, experienced and well trained technical staff in labs / workshops

W3. Less Faculty development programs & no development programs for Technical Staff.

W4. Student-Faculty ratio is poor & more than 15:1
W5. Less Industry Institute Interaction.
W6. Tendencies of absenteeism in the students.
W7. Director always busy in administrative work very less time to give directions to improve learning by students.
W8. Very few books are available on Ethics, Environment protection, personality development, soft/ communication skills & research activities.
W9. Limited titles of research journals available in library. E-journals take lot of down load time due to slow internet speed.
W10. Labs and Classrooms need modernization on regular basis.
W11. Limited number of hostel rooms.
W12. Less number Faculty members having Ph.D. and almost a few registered Ph.D. Guides.
W13. Insufficient number of separate cabins for faculty members.
W14. Inadequate central computing facilities. Internet bandwidth is inadequate.
W15. Faculty does not get adequate recharging / relaxing breaks during.
W16. Faculty is more focused towards teaching rather over-teaching instead of caring for quality of learning by the students.

Sample Opportunities:

O1. In Indian states Engg Colleges are allowed to charge more tuition fee for accredited BE programs.
O2. Accreditation shall attract more funds and sponsorship from AICTE & other funding agencies for establishing a finishing school, Entrepreneurship cum R&D and Innovation Centers.
O3. Growing economy is continually enhancing opportunities for better placement / employment both in institutes and industry.
O4. Potential is constantly growing to enhance Internal Revenue Generation (IRG) through R&D & Innovation projects from nearby industries.
O5. Projects like TEQIP are a great opportunity to embed Quality in our day to day services and transform any interested institute into an International Institute.

O6. Faculty with Ph.D. should be encouraged to register themselves as Ph.D. Guides and produce more PhDs from existing departments.

O7. Large number of AICTE/ UGC sponsored faculty development programs / conferences are being organized in nearby Engg Colleges. Local faculty can take advantage.

O8. Potentials for transforming MOUs into Operational relationships with national level institutes and industries located in and around the city.

O9. Provisions of Industry.

Sample Threats:

T1. Many seats are left vacant at the end of admission drive due to cut throat competition with other institutions at the national level.

T2. Mushrooming growth of Engg Colleges has resulted into shortage of competent faculty members.

T3. Retaining qualified and experienced faculty members has become a great problem for Engg Colleges.

T4. Theory centric examination system and rat race of awarding higher marks in sessional / term work is creating havoc in preparing employable graduates.

T5. Exponential growth of Engg Colleges or quantity has resulted into overall quality loss in technical education services.

T6. Voluntary NBA Accreditation is discouraging for adopting even minimum Quality assurance of services by Professional colleges.

T7. Technologies are developing fast and we have to change according to current trends and growing needs. Acquiring new technologies could be beyond our capacity.

T8. Learning-Teaching of emerging technologies is difficult due to lack of affordable text-books/ journals.

T9. Very often fast changes in the institution are being resisted by Political forces.

T10. Foreign Universities/ colleges may enter into already a cutthroat competition in a year or two.

T11. White collar jobs are being preferred by Engg Graduates which is resulting into non-availability of good scholars for PG programs.

T12. Talented scholars do not prefer careers in teaching profession.

2.4: EVOLVING SHARED VISION, MISSION AND VALUES:

Vision:

"People see things happening and ask why? I dream of things and ask why not?" **Robert Kennedy**

"Having a small aim is a crime" **APJ Abdul Kalam**

Vision is the future wishfully perceived by people who determine to grow in life. Visioning is the process by which the vision can be evolved. Vision indicates the destination where one wishes to reach within the frame work of available time and one's resolve & resourcefulness. In case of an institution or Department the ideal time frame can be 8 to 10 years. It is statement where a visionary manger resolves to develop with its institution or Department and reach to a targeted level.

"Vision creation is always a messy, difficult and sometimes emotionally charged exercise". **Prof. JP Kotter, Harward school**

The author recommends that the institute should hire the services of some experienced management development consultant for implementing the visioning process; however, some hints are given below to understand the visioning process.

Visioning process:

Step-1: Identify primary, secondary and tertiary stake holders and undertake SWOT analyses with them. Hold sessions with the stakeholders for mutual consultations and understanding their perceptions about the department and/ or the institute.

Step-2: Workout value analysis and value profiling of the department and the institution.

- Value = Valoir (French) = Worthiness/ to be of worth. Values are Ways of behaving to enable us to overcome hierarchical/ ego based diseases?
- How we would behave with each other? How we regard our customers, suppliers (of services) & community? How we respect the grey haired people?
- What limits we would not cross, come what may?

Sample statement of Values:

- o   Team working,
- o   Cost consciousness,
- o   Good house-keeping,
- o   Sincerity,
- o   loyalty,
- o   Integrity,
- o   Honesty,
- o   Commitment,
- o   Punctuality,
- o   Social responsibility,

Example: Values - IIT Delhi,

- o   Academic integrity and accountability.
- o   Respect and tolerance for the views of every individual.
- o   Attention to issues of national relevance as well as of global concern.
- o   Breadth of understanding, including knowledge of the human sciences.
- o   Appreciation of intellectual excellence and creativity.
- o   An unfettered spirit of exploration, rationality and enterprise.

Examples: Values, NITTTR, Bhopal,

- o   Respect for innovations and creativity,
- o   Cost, time and quality consciousness,
- o   Attitude of introspection,
- o   Discipline and punctuality,
- o   Honesty and Integrity and
- o   Social Responsibility.

Step-3: Conduct analyses of critical issues. These issues can be identified by considering the extreme situations such as combination of strength & opportunities and/ or weaknesses & threats.

Step-4: Formulate vision & Mission statements using nominal group technique or brain storming.

- **Vision statement** may indicate a destination, mission statements are ways & means to achieve vision to be implemented observing the scope of values to the utmost extent. Vision: "A vividly descriptive Image of what one wants to be or wants to be known for?"
- **Shared Vision:** "A picture of a preferred future state – that is grounded in a solid understanding of the business (Technical Education Service Provider), and is communicated in a way that inspires, motivates, and compels others to achieve it."

Evolving contents of vision statement:

- If we could be, what we wanted to be, what would we be ten years hence?
- Why the organization should continue to exist in future after ten years?
- What shall change and to what extent: Users, work priority and environment, redundant and new thrusts, emerging opportunities and threats?
- What impact are we likely to create on future partners and communities?
- What innovative services, we will provide to our customers ensuring not only their satisfaction but delight?

Examples

IIT Delhi;

Vision

To contribute to India and the World through excellence in scientific and technical education and research; to serve as a valuable resource for industry and society; and remain a source of pride for all Indians.

Mission

- To generate new knowledge by engaging in cutting-edge research and to promote academic growth by offering state-of-the-art undergraduate, postgraduate and doctoral programs.
- To identify, based on an informed perception of Indian, regional and global needs, areas of specialization upon which the institute can concentrate.
- To undertake collaborative projects which offer opportunities for long-term interaction with academia and industry.
- To develop human potential to its fullest extent so that intellectually capable and imaginatively gifted leaders can emerge in a range of professions.

CPSC Manila, Philippines-

- **Vision**: "Colombo Plan Staff College shall be a demand driven and self-reliant center of excellence in facilitating the creation of world class technicians oriented towards life-long learning and sustainable socio-economic development of member countries."

College of Engineering, Pune,

- **Vision:** To be a leader amongst engineering institutions in India, constantly pursuing excellence, and offering world class education with values.
- **Mission:** To pursue excellence in all facets of institute functioning.
- **Core Values**: "Quality and excellence in Education" at COEP bears witness to
  - o Excellence,
  - o Innovation,
  - o Ethics,
  - o Commitment,

Thus the future of the institute and departments manifest in terms of broader statements VISION, MISSION and VALUES. These broader statements become more pragmatic and achievable when they are derived in the light of SWOT analyses and /or perceptions of stakeholders about the program, department and institute as a whole as one entity.

Now, concentrate on two mandatory concepts for developing and implementing, sustaining OBTE and its accreditation. These are *Program Educational Objectives (PEOs) and Program (learning) Outcomes (POs).*

JN Technical University, Hyderabad, Telangana, India

- **Vision:** To provide for the advancement of learning and knowledge in Engineering & Technology, Physical and Social Sciences by teaching, research and experimentation or practical training or by such other means as the University may deem fit.

Anurag Engg College, Anantgiri, Nalgonda, AP,

- **Vision:** To be a premier Institute in the country and region for the study of Engineering, Technology and Management by maintaining high academic standards which promotes the analytical thinking and independent judgment among the prime stakeholders, enabling them to function responsibly in the globalized society.

Shri Sant Gajanan Maharaj College of Engg, Shegaon, MS

- **Vision:** To impart world-class Engineering and Management education in an environment of spiritual foundation to serve the global society.

IIT Mumbai, MS

- **Vision:** To be a fountainhead of new ideas and innovations in technology and Science.
- **Mission:** To create an ambience of academic excellence in which new ideas, research and scholarship flourish and from which the leaders and innovators of tomorrow emerge

2.5. PROGRAM EDUCATIONAL OBJECTIVES (PEOs):

The Program educational objectives are the broad statements that describe the expected achievements of graduates within first few years of their graduation from the program. *PEOs* can also be expressed in terms of indicators of the potential fields of employment & professional accomplishments within 3-4 years after graduation. The program objectives should be aligned to global or local needs, the vision of the institution, long term goals etc. For defining the program objectives the faculty members of the program must continuously work with local employers, industry and R&D advisors and the alumni. The **objectives** of the program can be broadly defined on five categories.

1. *Preparation*: To prepare students to excel in postgraduate programs or to succeed in industry/technical profession through global, rigorous education.

2. *Core Competence*: To provide students with a solid foundation in Mathematical, Scientific and Engineering fundamentals require to solve engineering problems and also to pursue higher studies.

3. *Breadth*: To train students with good scientific and engineering breadth so as to comprehend, analyze, design and create novel products and solution for the real life problems.

4. *Professionalism*: To inculcate in students professional and ethical attitude, effective communication skills, teamwork skills, multidisciplinary approach and ability to relate engineering issues to broader social context.

5. *Learning Environment*: To provide a student with an academic environment aware of excellence, leadership, written ethical codes and guidelines and the life-long learning needed for a successful professional career.

A few examples are given below to clarify the content implications of the concept of PEOs. One must distinguish that PEOs are the statements expressing the aspirations of the department offering the program indicating what kind of professionals shall be produced by pursuing the program and what kind of achievements can be expected out of these professionals after a few years acquiring graduation.

A-Bharat College of Engineering, Excellence Nagar

Program Educational Objectives (PEOs): BE Program

PEO 1: Produce electronics engineers with a strong practical and theoretical exposure in the relevant disciplines, which are able to contribute to society through innovation, enterprise and leadership.

PEO 2: To make students to workout solution to real life situations by using innovation, design, simulation, experimentation and testing hardware and software components.

PEO 3: To enable students to analyze and solve engineering problems by applying basic principles of mathematics, science and engineering and also able to use modern engineering techniques, skill and tools to fulfill need of society.

PEO 4: To nurture students with professional values, appropriate communication skills, teamwork spirit, inter-disciplinary approach in order to function in national, multinational organization as well as society.

PEO 5: To inculcate students to be sensitive to ethical, societal and environmental issues while conducting their professional duties.

Program Educational Objectives (PEOs) BE- Mechanical Engineering

1. To impart excellent education in Mechanical Engineering to have all-round development of students in order to serve the global society.

Other statements can be seen on website: **www.ssgmce.org**

B- Walchand Institute of Technology, Solapur, MS, India

Program Education Objectives: BE- Civil Engineering

1. To develop the technical ability amongst the students to synthesize data and technical concepts for application to civil engineering problems and projects.

2. To provide opportunity for students, to work as part of teams on multidisciplinary projects.

Other PEOs can be seen on website: www.witsolapur.org,

Analyses of PEOs by writing Implied sub-skills

For effective implementation, monitoring and assessment of intended abilities of graduates within PEOs should be broken down in to the implied skills. The following example illustrates how abilities implied in a few PEOs can be broken down into implied skills. This shall help in identifying indicators/ criteria & for setting up goals to assess the achievement of PEOs.

PEO-1: **Ability to undertake R&D tasks and present seminar of findings.**

Skill -1.1: Exploring Cause and Effect relationship and analyzing the problem.

Skill -1.2: Arriving at a tentative solution and writing a report of the project using modern software tools & simulation.

Skill -1.3: Presenting and defending a seminar of the R&D work.

PEO-2: **Ability to design and conduct a developmental tests on the prototype of the designed product / process.**

Skill 2.1: Design a product / process considering profession relevant aspects and variable, using modern design tools and software systems.

Skill 2.2: Draft technical drawings for producing a prototype product/ process.

Skill 2.3: Conduct developmental tests for evaluating acceptability of the outcome against predefined criteria.

Skill 2.4: Present a seminar to defend the design results.

PEO 3: **Ability to undertake process planning and to manage manufacturing of a given product or process, and related resources and targets.**

Skill 3.1: Conduct process planning for manufacturing of a given product or process

Skill 3.2: Set up the manufacturing systems and manage the manufacturing process.

Skill 3.3: Undertake quality assurance procedures in order to ensure compliance with the product / process specifications with enterprising spirit.

PEO 4: **Ability to manage marketing and distribution of products of a business enterprise with entrepreneurship**

Skill 4.1: Design a marketing strategies/ policies and appoint distributors of your product and services.

Skill 4.2: Appoint logistics partners and transport net work

Skill 4.3: Establish the net-work of spares and consumables and customer feedback systems

PEO 5: **Ability to undertake and manage erection and commissioning of a system at site of its use.**

Skill 5.1: Organize an erection team & erection works after initial survey of sites and location topography

Skill 5.2: Organize Commissioning of system after selecting a competent team and meet operational requirements and satisfy customers before handing over the system.

Skill 5.3: Negotiate after sales terms and conditions for future interactions and transactions.

PEO 6: **Ability to design and implement after sales maintenance & condition monitoring of the supplied system at client's site with entrepreneurship**

Skill 6.1: Work out the preventive and corrective maintenance schedules, policies and suggest the inventory of spares and consumables which should be maintained at site.

Skill 6.2: Establish the channels of communication between customers, service agency and the main supplier and related feedback system.

Skill 6.3: Inspect the facilities of the service center and provide suggestions to improve the productivity and quality of services maintaining the entrepreneurship spirit.

Please note that the PEOs should reflect what the department should be doing to develop students in to professional graduates those who will accomplish excellence in their profession (fast career growth and holding key positions just after 3 to 4 years after graduations) and who are likely to contribute more in some projected stream of the profession or specific areas of research design and development or academic fields. A better way to write these should be in terms what the service provider will do to ensure accomplishment of PEOs. This logic shall make identification of indicators of accomplishment of PEOs so that better assessment shall become possible.

One of the basic requirements of producing highly professional graduates is to transform the existing faculty members in highly committed professional who are capable of becoming ROLE MODELS of one or more students. According to Bandura's Social Leaning theory, a large number of attitudes get transferred without any deliberate efforts on the part of the faculty members.

2.6: PROGRAM (LEARNING) OUTCOMES (POs)

For a graduate, POs indicate knowledge, skills and attitudinal behaviors acquired by the students at the time of graduation. The outcomes essentially indicate what a student can do using different subject-based knowledge & skills acquired while undergoing the program. They should be aligned with Global Graduate Attributes or GAs so as to facilitate & ensure global mobility. **Student or Program (Learning) Outcomes or POs** describe what students are expected to know and be able to do by the time of graduation. These relate to the skills, knowledge, and behaviors that students acquire as they progress through the program.

Engineering is an activity that is essential to meeting the needs of people, economic development and the provision of services to society. Engineering involves the purposeful application of mathematical and natural sciences and a body of engineering knowledge, technology and techniques.

GAs or POs indicate Knowledge base and personality attributes to enable the graduate to continue learning and to proceed to formative development that will develop the competencies required for independent practice. Graduate attributes form a set of individually assessable outcomes that are the components indicative of the graduate's potential to acquire competence to practice at the appropriate level. The graduate attributes are exemplars of the attributes expected of graduate from an accredited program. Graduate attributes are clear, succinct statements of the expected capability, qualified if necessary by a range indication appropriate to the type of program.

International Engineering Alliance (IEA) GAs or Washington Accord GAs for BE or B Tech programs are given below.

WA-1.   **Engineering knowledge:** Knowledge of mathematics, natural science, engineering fundamentals and an engineering specialization respectively to the solution of complex engineering problems

WA-2.   **Problem Analysis:** Identify, formulate, research literature and analyze complex engineering problems reaching substantiated conclusions using first principles of mathematics, natural sciences and engineering sciences.

WA-3.   **Design/ Development of Solutions**: Design solutions for complex engineering problems and design system components or processes that meet specified needs with appropriate consideration for public health and safety, cultural, societal and environmental considerations.

WA-4.   **Investigation:** Conduct investigations of complex problems using research-based knowledge and research methods including design of experiments, analysis and interpretation of data and synthesis of information to provide valid conclusions.

WA-5.   **Modern Tool Usage:** Create, select and apply appropriate techniques, resources and modern engineering and IT tools including prediction and modeling to complex engineering activities with an understanding of the limitations.

WA-6.   **The Engineer and Society**: Apply reasoning informed by contextual knowledge to assess societal, health, safety, legal and cultural issues and the consequent responsibilities relevant to professional engineering practice.

WA-7.   **Environment and Sustainability:** Understand the impact of professional engineering solutions in societal and environmental contexts and demonstrate knowledge of and need for sustainable development.

WA-8.   **Ethics:** Apply ethical principles and commit to professional ethics and responsibilities and norms of engineering practice.

WA-9.   **Individual and Team work**: Function effectively as an individual, and as a member or leader in diverse teams and in multi-disciplinary settings.

WA-10. **Communication:** Communicate effectively on complex engineering activities with the engineering community and with society at large, such as being able to comprehend and write effective reports and design documentation, make effective presentations, and give and receive clear instructions.

WA-11. **Project management and Finances:** Demonstrate knowledge and understanding of engineering management principles and economic decision – making and apply these to one's own work, as a member and leader in a team, to manage projects and in multidisciplinary environments.

WA-12. **Lifelong Learning**: Recognize the need for, and have the preparation and ability to engage in independent and life - long learning in the broadest context of technological change.

Each BE or B tech 4 years engineering program shall have comparable Program Outcomes but in the context of different professional specializations. Two statements of POs have been given below to clarify the content implications of the POs belonging to different specializations.

A: Shri Sant Gajanan Maharaj College of Engineering- Program Outcomes (POs):

Program Outcomes (POs): BE-Electronic Communication Engg.

1. Graduates will demonstrate knowledge of mathematics, science and engineering in appropriate fields of Electronics & Tele-communication engineering practice.

Other statements can be seen on their website: **www.ssgmce.org**

Other example of Program Outcomes (POs) of a BE program is provided below:
1. An ability to apply knowledge of mathematics, science, and engineering.
2. An ability to design and conduct experiments, as well as to analyze and interpret data.

3. An ability to design a system, component or process to meet desired needs within realistic constraints of real life problems catering the needs of industry and society.
4. An ability to function in multi-disciplinary teams.
5. An ability to identify, formulate and solve engineering problems.
6. An understanding of professional and ethical responsibility.
7. An ability to communicate effectively and professionally through oral, written and graphical media.
8. The broad education necessary to understand the impact of engineering solutions in a global, economic, environmental and societal context.
9. Recognition of the need for, and an ability to engage in life-long learning.
10. Knowledge of contemporary issues.
11. An ability to use measurement techniques, analysis techniques, skills and modern engineering tools necessary for engineering practice
12. Commitment to quality, timeliness, and continuous improvement

One Program Outcome (PO)-BE- Civil Engg. of another engg college is given below;

o   Graduates will demonstrate an ability to design a civil engineering structure / project acceptable and useful to society that meets desired specifications and requirements.

You can find many more examples when you shall explore websites of many Asian and American Technical Institutions.

Relationships of different concepts manifesting the aspirations for excellence of an educational enterprise:

The figure 2.2 illustrates the intimate relationship and mutual dependency of different formats of expressions of aspirations of the institute indicating the quality Assurance of the professional education being imparted to its students and also the kind of professional graduates expected to be produced. COs stand for Course Outcomes. **Course Outcomes** are clear statements of what a student should be able to demonstrate upon completion of a course. Examples of COs shall be given in further chapters at appropriate place.

This diagram makes one thing very clear that the earlier practice of writing using very attractive words and phrases must be avoided. Whatever statements you shall write need to influence all other inferior concepts and we should be able to find out suitable indicators to assess them and report the degree of success in achieving these concepts in true spirit and make records of evidences to feel proud and share with others with a pleasant feeling of our own achievements.

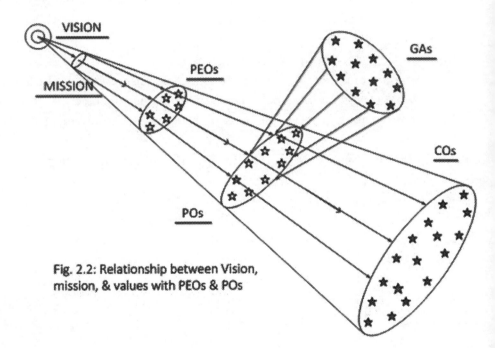

Fig. 2.2: Relationship between Vision, mission, & values with PEOs & POs

CHAPTER 3.0

INNOVATIONS FOR QUALITY IMPROVEMENT

3.1. Rationale

3.2. Improving Governance

3.3. Improving Autonomy: four autonomies

3.4. Innovative Faculty & Staff Development

3.5. Innovative Learning & Teaching Methods

3.6. Innovations in Students' Assessment

3.7. Innovations in Industry- Institute Partnership

3.8. R&D, entrepreneurship and Consultancy center

3.1: RATIONALE

Govt. of India has been focusing on quality improvement since 1980. It launched World Bank Assisted Quality Improvement programs for Polytechnic Colleges under the name Tech-Ed I through Tech ED-IV and assisted 25 state Governments and UTs during the period from 1991 to 2007. In 2002-03 GoI gave attention to Degree level Technical Education by launching the World Bank Assisted Project under the title 'Technical Education Quality Improvement Program (TEQIP).' Each of its three phases of TEQIP-I, II and III will have a duration of about 4 to 5 years. During phase –I about 127 colleges were covered from 13 states. TEQIP-II (2010-14) is continuing in about 150+ colleges.

It is not possible to assist all the needy Engineering and Polytechnic colleges under such externally funded projects. However, the need of launching such quality improvement projects is sufficient proof that there is a dire need of improving operations of majority of Technical and other Professional institutions.

About 75 to 80% of total Engg. & Polytechnic colleges in India are owned by private societies and they are operating in self-financing mode. The tuition fee needs to be high enough to meet their operational cost. The customer students of these educational enterprises have every right to demand quality services and better employability skills imparted to them. Most residents of global village and fraternity of professional educators have very well realized that maintaining the high quality of products & services is the only weapon to face the cut throat war of survival of every enterprise in a depressing economic environment.

The management of these institutions knows that WTO has already classified educational organizations as a service Industry in Jan 2005. It is moral and ethical responsibility of every commercial educational enterprise that they care for proper satisfaction of their customers. The market driven economy induces one more responsibilities that the functional requirements of products & services should be driven by the market needs rather than by the whims of the producer or provider.

The following information has been composed to assist the management and faculty of the institute to share ideas in brief to induce quality improvement in self-help mode. Many ideas have been tried by the author while he was advisor TEQIP and facilitator in other Quality Assurance projects in many institutions. It is hoped that interested institutes shall find some of these ideas useful for quality improvement efforts of their institutes. The broader hints of these ideas need to be expanded further by the managers and the faculty of the institute commensurate with their choices and situations.

3.2: IMPROVING GOVERNANCE:

Many private self-financing technical institutions belong to a large group of institutions teaching different specializations of Art, Science and Technology. They are governed by a single board of management or the owner of the society or group. The on spot decisions made are mostly depend upon the whims of a one or two less educated owners or business-persons of the society. These owners may not be aware of the complexities and background information and are often likely to take wrong decisions which may prove to be detrimental to their own interests, in the long run. It is therefore highly desirable that policy making decisions should be based on well informed discussions which are undertaken in the presence of some experienced & knowledgeable persons who should also be stakeholders of the institute and are functioning as accountable members of Board of Management or Governors. As per UGC and AICTE guidelines the following is the constitution of a Board of Governors of a Technical Institution.

In many institutions the owners have their identified favorite faculty or other employees who pass on biased information and keep them away from the truth of the situations. The owners should remove all such communication barriers and should establish direct communication links with sincere and committed employees who can tell boldly the reality and suggestions for right decision making.

Members of Board of Governors of a Private Engg/ Polytechnic College

*5 Members: Management Trust or management as per the constitution or bye-laws, with the Chairman or President / Director as the Chairperson. (Or 3 members: in case of Govt. or Govt. aided or Autonomous Institution)

*2 Members: Faculty of the institution Nominated by the Principal, based on seniority

*1 Member: Educationist or Industrialist Nominated by the Management

*1 Member: UGC/ AICTE nominee Nominated by the UGC/AICTE

*1 Member: State Government or DTE's nominee Academician not below the rank of Professor or State Government official, of Directorate of Higher Education/ State Council of Higher Education

*1 Member: University nominee Nominated by the affiliating University

*1 Member & Secretary: Director or Principal of institution Ex-officio who also functions as secretary of the BoG and proposes agenda and keeps records of the minutes of the meetings. He takes action

on the decisions by the BoG as well as submits action taken report of actions taken during the last few months lapsed after the previous meeting of BoG.

Board of Governors of the institutions shall have powers to:

- Fix the fees and other charges payable by the students of the institution on the recommendations of the Finance Committee.
- Approve institution of scholarships, fellowships, studentships, medals, prizes and certificates on the recommendations of the Academic Council.
- Approve institution of new programs of study leading to Degrees and/ or Diplomas.
- Perform such other functions and institute such committees, as may be necessary and deemed fit for the proper development, and fulfill the objectives for which the institution has been declared as autonomous.
- Evolve the policies & rules regarding the delegation of autonomy to the functionaries of the institute and approve guidelines for effective implementation of the autonomies.
- Monitor scientifically the performance of the institute and fix responsibilities for deterioration of quality of services if desirable.

3.3: IMPROVING FOUR AUTONOMIES:

Autonomy is the capacity of a rational individual to make an informed, un-coerced decision. Quality is in itself a big thing but this big thing quality can only be achieved by undertaking many small things or actions. It cannot be implemented only by management by issuing orders or making certain rules and procedures. Quality consciousness is an attitude which comes slowly over a period of time by persistent efforts by one and all the functionaries. Discussions for clarifications, orientation and training can be helpful in the initial stage. But, functionaries need to act more in accordance to their commitments & convictions towards improving their individual services along with the institutional services as a whole.

The subsystems need to be installed which operate in self-correcting mode. It means that all the functionaries should try to take rational decisions and act within their autonomy limits.

The BoG need to resolve to delegate powers in phased manner and enhance the limits of autonomy, responsibility and accountability awarded to all stakeholders / employees from Chairperson to the sweeper. Every autonomy & related issues cannot be written on paper, but if it is practiced continuously as a part of work culture or ethics, it shall be internalized as a tradition. Quality improvement is long drawn endeavor which comes only by mutual respect and feelings of adjustments in the best interest of the institution and its customers.

Quality assurance is a matter related to attitude and feelings in the heart. It cannot be initiated and sustained unless employees are committed and convinced from the depth of their heart. So, one should not hope that the quality assurance can be installed simply by orders and circulars of the director or chairpersons. Higher management must first commit to the caring attitude towards the customers and employees before expecting their commitment to quality assurance.

Four categories of Autonomy:

a. **Managerial Autonomy**
b. **Academic Autonomy**
c. **Administrative Autonomy**
d. **Financial Autonomy**

Managerial Autonomy:

The managers of the institute who are directly responsible for the managing academic quality of the education services are the Director/ Principal, Deans, Registrar, Accounts Officer and the Head of the Academic Departments. They are managing the affairs of the institute and the department respectively. They must be delegated adequate autonomy in phases so that they keep on taking many small steps without getting approval for a minor decisions or actions as per guidelines developed for quality assurance. Managerial Autonomy shall involve appointing subordinate employees, giving rewards and incentives or certificate of appreciation for outstanding performance, defining duties & responsibilities of a Dean, Registrar, Accounts officer, Professor and Assistant Professor and other staff etc. Monitoring the progress of the implementation, proper record keeping of evidences of achievements and using them in marketing the services as and when necessary.

Academic Autonomy:

Decisions related to modifying curriculum, reforming assessment procedures and criteria, preparing academic calendar, Learning -Teaching strategies, students & programs' assessment methods & instruments, selecting faculty to teach a particular subject or practical work or R&D project work etc., analyzing students' feedback and suggesting corrective measure to the faculty, suggesting suitable learning-teaching method or media, planning and assessing an academic achievement etc. shall fall in the category of academic autonomy. For initiating and sustaining quality assurance in an educational institution, academic autonomy is the key success factor.

Presently the personal autonomy of a faculty in higher education is very high. It needs to be regulated for effective implementation of outcome based education. There is need for more cooperation and coordination amongst departmental and interdepartmental faculty for integrated assessment of Program outcomes. This coordination shall become quite critical while certifying those POs for which the affiliating university shall not have data as well as authority of certification. However, the affiliating university should provide agreement in principle for all reforms required to nurture quality assurance and improvement.

Academic autonomy is very critical factor for implementing outcome based education because non-autonomous institute does not have power to make or modify curriculum of the program. Therefore, NBA has recommended to appoint a number of persons to perform academic functions and leave all managerial and administrative decisions in the hands of HoDs. **Program Coordinator** should be responsible for all academic decisions in the department related to a specific program. The institute through program coordinator can only modify the existing syllabi by adding a few topics and assignments to achieve PEOs & POs. So the questions such as, 'how much autonomy HoD & Senior faculty will have in such academic matters?', and 'to what extent a department has to maintain the consistency with the general institutional academic framework of curriculum development'. It becomes important to strike a balance between the individuality of a department, its vision & mission and vision & missions of the institute.

Academic positions recommended by NBA related to offering a program;

- **Department advisory board or DAB**: to support, monitor & award approval to quality assurance proposals of the faculty
- **Program Coordinator**: to manage support, design and implementation of all academic reforms to achieve PEOs and POs
- **Program Assessment Committee or PAC**: to suggest and improve assessment systems, policies, rules, instruments, record keeping, and certification's bases and maintaining individual assessment records of each student and parameter needed for course, program and institutional evaluation.
- **Module Coordinator**: Maintaining consistencies amongst the faculty members facilitating delivery of courses pertaining to a cluster / module.
- **Course Coordinator:** When a single common course is taught by many faculty members, one of the faculty member shall nominated to act as coordinator who shall maintain consistency in learning-teaching and assessment of the students & the course.

Administrative Autonomy: Regulating the expected performance of employees, punctuality, preparing salary bills, keeping record of appointment and promotions etc. and granting short leaves on genuine grounds, making arrangements to substitute faculty on leave, taking care of attendance & recording in the database etc., Conducting admission drive, maintaining personal records of students and all other human resources along with their individual rewards and penalties.

Financial Autonomy: Power to spend funds of the institute commensurate with the budget provisions within the set limits, for a purpose satisfying the best interest of the institute can be explained as financial autonomy. The financial autonomy has to be tapered down with the reducing level of the employees. Chairman shall have the maximum financial power, Director& HoDs shall have lesser powers, and even the faculty in-charge a lab may also have some financial power for improving overall effectiveness of operations of the institute and services.

In most of the private institute most autonomies are vested in the chairperson of the institute who also owns the institute fully or partially. Some guidelines should be circulated to enabling take rational & justifiable decisions by all subordinate functionaries. It is recommended that the management should evolve the plan for delegation of autonomy and accountability considering the need of the operations as well as enhancing the learning opportunities by students as well as faculty and staff.

3.4: INNOVATIVE FACULTY AND STAFF DEVELOPMENT

Shortage of well-trained & competent faculty and staff is the most worrying factor for the management of the majority of institutions. The only option left is to develop whatever human resources are available with the institute. The quality of faculty and the technical staff directly influences the quality of learning & services of the institute. It is therefore essential that the management devises innovative approaches for continually developing the existing faculty and staff.

Which one of the following approaches shall be useful in your circumstances, needs to be tried out with open mind?

- Self-development Group approach,
- Peers' & Students' feedback based Performance appraisal & Development
- Incentives schemes Linked to Self-appraisal with & incidental assessment
- Need based short-term orientation & training programs

Self-development Group approach,

It is based upon the assumptions that the group wisdom is much greater that individual wisdom. This approach may be beneficial to both faculty and students. The approach is quite simple.

- Faculty or staff or students choose persons by mutual consent to form a small group of 3 to 5 members. They decide to share their functional difficulties in an informal way as and when they have an opportunity to meet with each other. Opportunities may be; taking lunch or snacks, playing sports, gossiping in parking area, sudden meeting in a market or walking in a corridor.

- Faculty can share teaching difficulties & plans to overcome, contents and design of slides for a presentation. Lab staff may discuss the problem of repairing an equipment and problems of developing a new experimental setup. Students may share the learning difficulties of a confusing topic or solving problems belonging to a home or library assignment & so on.

- They can also maintain a logbook to record lessons learned during a semester from a self-development group experimentation. Brief reports of such experiences may also be shared in a departmental seminar organized once a semester.

Peers' & Students' feedback based Performance appraisal & Development

The performance of all teaching faculty and staff should be appraised by their customer students. Peers and superiors may also be asked to provide feedback on the performance of the teaching faculty and staff.

Peers' Feedback: The feedback from supervisor HoD and one or two selected senior peers may be asked once or twice in a semester to give feedback on the basis of mutually agreed upon criteria. These criteria should have focus on those aspects which directly enhance quality of learning. The weightage of all other criteria related to punctuality, discipline and administrative aspects should be less than weightage of academic criteria.

The concerned faculty need to provide permission to supervisors or senior faculty and peers to make surprise visits to his/her classrooms and labs for making incidental observations of the quality of interactions / transactions with students. The criteria for feedback need to be developed giving preference to those activities which promote learning.

Students' Feedback: the students' feedback is the most valuable feedback for quality improvement in the services of the institute. The students' learning is the fundamental purpose of the existence of the institute. It is not necessary to collect feedback from all the students, but to receive feedback from a 50% sample. Sampling shall reduce the size of data to be processed, yet does not make much compromise to project true feelings of the students.

The number of feedback criteria should be limited and should not take more than five minutes to respond. An example of set of criteria are given below.

1. Punctuality in coming & going to the class.
2. Knowledge / Expertise in the subject taught
3. Clarity of oral communication and Interaction with students
4. Effective Communication using media (Chalkboard, OHP-Transparencies, Power Point slides, models, Educational Games, Animations, Simulations etc.)
5. Motivation in the beginning and Speed of teaching – faster / slower / proper / most proper.
6. Assignments/ Unit Tests or numerical problems given as class work & home work.
7. Completing all units in the syllabus as per Course plan
8. Overall impression on the basis of guidance given to you in Lab, Tutorials, Model Questions, Assignments, Extra Classes, and as TG)

If possible, provide some space in the feedback sheet so that student can write open remarks.

The feedback from different respondents such as students, supervisors, peers should be compiled with different weights allocated to the feedback of different respondents. For instance weights for students' feedback mar be 60%, 20% each for feedbacks of supervisor and peers.

The collated and combined feedback % may become criteria for deciding the incentives and rewards.

Suggested IT Solution: The Department of IT & CSE of any Engg College are capable of developing a suitable software as students' major projects to perform the following functions related to receiving, processing and generate reports for initiating further action;

• Whenever a student shall login, it can provide feedback in the digital format appearing on the screen of the PC. The selected students can login in any PC of a computer lab within the working hours of the institute on specified days.

- The software shall process the data after a specified day & time and generate a soft report of the weighted average rating against each criteria and the overall rating of the concerned teacher.
- If required a visual report should also be generated in the form of bar chart or performance radar.

The IT solution shall improve the efficiency as well as effectiveness of the feedback system.

Incentive schemes Linked to Self-appraisal & with incidental assessment

Some examples of the incentive schemes which can be used for teaching faculty and staff are listed below;

- Financial incentive:
    - o Extra increments in addition to Regular increments in salary.
    - o Lump-sum cash reward for achieving some difficult performance

- Recognition by Certification:
    - o Best Teacher & Technician award during a semester- certificate with some token gift.
    - o Recognition of performance by letters of appreciation, citation in the publications of the institute and financial incentives some times.

- Academic Sponsorship to participate in;
    - o Regional/national short-term training program or workshops
    - o A regional & national conferences
    - o An international conferences
    - o Study visits to other universities or Institutions.

- Career Growth: Appointing on higher positions of importance as a reward for better productivity and quality services.

Objective assessment should be used to decide the quality and quantum of incentives to be given to selected employee. One of the most effective instruments is the self-assessment-report or Self-appraisal-report (SAR). SAR should be collected once in a year. The following example provides the information which may be collected from faculty members in the format of SAR.

1. Personal bio-data
2. Teaching load in hours per week during odd / even semester = 8%
3. Course material provided: tutorials, assignments, question bank = 8%
4. Course files finalized and submitted or revised = 5%
5. Development and use of learning resources = 8%
6. Use of innovative teaching learning strategies= 8%
7. SWOT analysis of self. = 5%
8. Students' performance in internal mid-semester tests/university. Exams = 8%
9. Your analysis & comments on university results = 2%
10. Attendance of students (average % for a semester) = 8%
11. Awards won / honor (s) conferred on you / special assignments at the university, in-charge of institute exams, text books or special scripts written, papers written and published, review of books = 10%
12. Fulfillment of co-curricular and extra-curricular tasks = 11%
    - Regular daily reporting = 1%,
    - Regular counseling of students by tutor guardian = 2%
    - Lab development work = 2%,
    - Examination management = 2%
    - Organizing extra-curricular activities (events/workshops) = 1%
    - Organization of innovative assessment & record keeping = 2%
13. Member of task groups = 6%
    - Value Addition Courses for better employment = 2%,
    - Organizing Students' Training for Campus Placement = 2%,
    - organizing training of 50 students = 2%
14. Average students' feedback (ASFB) rating for the last semester = 8%
15. Overall self-evaluation rating as a teacher = 5%
16. Areas in which you would like to receive advance training ether to overcome your weaknesses or supplement your expertize to prepare for future changes.

Such criteria can be formulated to assess the overall performance rating of the faculty or staff. SAR shall also indicate all the strengths and weaknesses of the person. Considering every aspect the overall rating can be estimated.

PADS: Need based short-term orientation & training programs

After going through all complete profile and performance of a person the Director can recommend for both 1. Incentives for outstanding performance and 2. Short term orientation and training program to be organized in-house or by an outside agency. Such an approach where a particular group of trainees are selected for a typical training program or orientation program or counselling appointment with a clinical psychologist seems to be most beneficial to all the stake holders. Need-based development is also known as Performance based Appraisal and Development System (PADS).

PADS also satisfies the broader needs of the adult learning and proper use of the expertise of the participating trainees. The acceptance of such program is normally quite high which ensure far better learning as compared to training programs forced on them by the management on the basis of ad-hock decision.

3.5: INNOVATIVE CLASSROOM LEARNING AND TEACHING (L-T) METHODS:

Earlier it was a practice to call teaching-learning methods. Author suggests that we should call this phrase as Learning-teaching methods. The difference in the two phrase is only the process of focus or higher preference. In the author's approach the emphasis has been given on learning which basic purpose of education & training is.

The methods having focus of learning shall make students more involved in the process of interaction with the teacher or other physical resources. The methods where students are passive listeners or observers and teacher is more active then only teachers learns then subject matter much better than the earlier level.

Some of the following methods should be encouraged in the higher education sector for better learning by students in the contact mode of educational institute.

Large group methods (51 to 100 students)

- Highly participative Lecture cum discussion method
- Classroom demonstrations by students of simpler experiments of labs, along with teaching of related theory
- Seminar Method
- Panel Discussion Method

Medium Group Methods (30 to 50)

- Classroom Seminar by students method
- Classroom demonstrations by students method
- Industrial visits method
- General Tutorial Method
- Group discussion methods
- Case study methods
- Laboratory/ Workshop Demonstration method

Small Group Method (10 to 20)

- Open ended design problem solving tutorial
- Case study method
- Micro & Minor project method

Micro group method (1 to 10)

- Micro and minor project methods
- Major Graduation Project & Report Method
- Industrial visits and training method followed by report writing and group presentation method.
- Industrial action research and Dissertation method.

The following methods are more popular in most of the institutions of higher education because of the commercial consideration and low cost. Such methods are also the major reason for lower quality of learning but nobody seems to bother about learning particularly in private educational enterprises.

It often happens because the managers had no opportunities in their life to experience the taste of higher quality in world class institutions. Perhaps the person who has designed the business model of such enterprises have also not tasted the higher returns on investment on quality assurance however it takes longer periods for returns to realize.

As a reforms, since the amount of learning is relatively less therefore management of the institutions and the affiliating university should in general discourage the use of such methods.

- Monologue Lecture method
- Monotonous Lecture method with media without participation of students
- Tutorial method in large groups of more than 20 students.

Quality & Creativity: The author is not suggesting that current L-T practices being followed are completely ineffective. Some gifted teachers have capabilities to transform any classroom environment into a highly charged leaning climate and students never miss such classes if such teachers are available in the college. The innovations should be made by a teacher itself using its creativity so that;

1. The quality of learning improves which can be seen on the faces of the students at the end of the session.
2. The quality of learning depends upon the amount of enthusiasm of the teacher who wishes to facilitate learning by stretching itself to the maximum, yet at the same time, maintaining the calmness in the minds of learners.
3. The quality of learning by adult students improves by involving students in planning the content and delivery processes of L-T sessions occasionally and assuring them that the content they are learning is quite relevant to the needs of their future careers. So the teacher often should connect the content with future career requirements and upcoming opportunities/ threats.
4. Never forget that you are dealing with adults and they feel in the similar ways as you feel while interacting with them. So always maintain a

boundary of mutual respect, a safe distance and avoid at all costs humiliating any adult in front other adults.

5. When teacher cares for future of students, respects and recognizes their individual strengths, the future of teacher shall automatically shine without failure.

3.5.1: The Classroom Seminar Method:

The salient features about most of the methods mentioned above are available in the literature. The classroom seminar method has been practiced by the author himself as well as by his trainee teachers very effectively and therefore sharing some of its typical features shall be desirable here. This is one of the very potential methods which compels students to learn the content as well as practice the employability skills. It is highly recommended for implementing OBTE.

Basic idea: the teacher gives self-study assignment to students and later on students present seminar within the classroom itself during the time allocated for the class is the classroom seminar. However, more detailed steps for organizing the CR Seminar are given below as guidelines for the interested teachers;

- **Step-1**: Teacher should select a simpler but highly descriptive topic which can easily be learned by a normal student if they study it with some care & attention. It can be any other topic which has lower self-learning difficulty. Divide the topic into 4 sub-topics.

- **Step-2:** Make 10 small groups of 60 students having 6 members in each group. Allocate the four sub-topics to four selected small groups.

- **Step-3:** Each sub-group shall perform the assignment in 3 micro-groups (MG).

  o MG-1 shall do research on the topic and search material available in the text book, websites, intranet and internet. They compile relevant material and handover to MG-2. MG-1 should keep a logbook and record its activities with date & time.

    o   MG-2 shall write brief notes of about 1 to 2 pages and make a power point presentation of about 7 to 9 slides. They handover the material to MG-3.

    o   One person from MG-3 shall make presentation on specifies date & time and the other person shall handle questions and answers. The total presentation & discussion time available is 10 minutes.

    o   These roles can be slightly changed by teacher if desired and should be rotated during subsequent seminars.

- **Step-4:** The teacher at the end of 4 presentations of about 10 minutes each should conclude the seminar by pointing out strengths of each group and also pointing out salient weaknesses / mistakes committed by these groups.
- **Step-5:** the teacher shall assess the performance of each group on the basis of the preparations, content, confidence, labor inputs and novelty in presentation. The assessment grades are made known through a notice pasted on Departments' notice board within a week.
- **Step-6:** The best seminar of the semester within the course should be rewarded by the class teacher to make the seminar competitive and challenging.

The teachers using CR-Seminar method shall realize immense benefits & improvements in the overall performance and personalities of the students of its class.

3.5.2: The Classroom Demonstration Method

In case of Laboratory based instruction, the author made the following observations while working on potential innovations for quality assurance in both Engineering and Polytechnic colleges.

- Many experiments are performed by small group of students which are meant only for verifying certain theoretical principles regularly taught in the classrooms. These experiments are not very challenging to students and can be performed within half of the time allocated for lab session. The innovative teacher can easily convert such experiments in to classroom demonstration sessions.

- If out of 10 experiments even if 3 to 4 can be transformed into interactive/ participative classroom demonstrations, then you shall save about 2 weeks Lab sessions even after doing two classroom demonstrations every week.

- These extra lab sessions which available on 2 saved weeks can be used for performing more complex and problem solving type experiments or design oriented micro projects in the labs. Thus this innovation makes it possible for transferring some problem solving skills implied in POs.

On the bases of analyses similar to one mentioned above using classroom demonstration can become quite popular amongst innovative teachers. Since Classroom demonstration results into learning outcomes better than the earlier traditional approach, some of the features of this method are elaborated below for the benefits of teachers who would like to pursue some similar innovation.

Features of Classroom Demonstration

- The integration of teaching sessions of theoretical principles along with the sessions of classroom demonstration, substituting some of the simpler lab experiments, is highly desirable condition to make learning more productive and long-term.

- Learning by students will enhance when teacher shall involve them in planning and implementation of the demonstration. So the plan for demo needs to include a lot of activities left for students to execute. Some sample activities may be; operating the equipment as per instructions by the teacher, taking readings, adjusting the instruments and minimizing the errors in observations of variable parameters, computing the results, manipulating the video equipment used as magnifying system for small components and indicators/ dials & so on.

- Class demonstrations present a lot of opportunities for satisfying the emotional needs of adolescent persons transiting into adulthood. These youth are in constant search of challenging tasks to prove their mite and get recognition amongst peers. Many attitudinal personality attributes can be modified by encouraging use of methods which enhance participation of students.

- Most of the laboratory appliances are made of smaller size and there visibility and legibility is decided on the basis of a viewing distance of about 2 to 3 meters. The viewing distance of a normal classroom demonstration varies from 4 to 13 meters. So when we wish to use normal lab appliances for classroom demonstrations, we must ensure the clear visibility of those smaller features of the appliance which clarifies the concepts and processes being demonstrated and being applied in causing the effects.

- Amongst many options to ensure clear visibility of smaller parts, use of one or two dedicated video camera with video signal outputs fed to LCD projector seems to be most convenient and economical. LCD projector shall magnify the picture by 5 to 8 times with adequate brightness and clarity. Properly selected low wattage lighting should be adequate to produce a bright picture of the appliance. One camera may show the whole setup and the second one may show the close-ups. A simple camera switching device can be used. One multimedia teaching room in each department can be the most effective ways to integrate classroom demonstrations with regular teaching sessions.

3.5.3 Lab & Workshop based Methods:

The Laboratories & work-shops based learning is traditionally termed as experiment. In fact in the real sense, all the practical learning activities cannot be classified as experiments. Therefore, the practical learning in the Labs & workshops is termed as experience rather than experiment. These experiences impart skills related to applications of concepts, principles, techniques and technologies. Such learning experiences occur in the Laboratories and workshops.

Some of the following innovations can be experimented in both Labs & workshops to begin with. Let the individual and small group creativity of teachers play its role in interpreting and implementing the ideas explained below in brief;

- Performing a variety of experiments with graded challenges or difficulties for students. Experience related to;

  a. Measuring properties of a particular system or element.
  b. Comprehending attributes of concepts
  c. Verifying scientific & Engineering laws and principles
  d. Determination of effects of changes in parameters of a given system.
  e. Analysis & synthesis of a system
  f. Manipulative techniques or operational skills
  g. Problem solving and or designing abilities (by doing a task = to micro project)

- Transferring simpler experiments to classroom as classroom demonstrations. (already explained earlier)
- Developing assessment rubrics for different types of experiences and tuning them with Program Outcomes (POs)
- Developing Lab & Workshop Manuals explaining; general philosophy of practical learning activities within a semester, specific objectives of each experience, specific tasks to be performed by the students, specific criteria assessment of learning outcomes, planning on the part of both teachers and students before undergoing a practical learning experience etc.

3.5.4: Innovative Micro, Minor and Major Project Work Experiences

Learning experiences of doing a problem solving projects of different difficulty levels at different semesters of studies during an Engg program is a very critical and unavoidable activity intended to train every graduate to acquire an interdisciplinary open ended problem solving ability, using the time available during all the contact semesters.

The **micro projects** are problem solving experience which cut across 3 to 5 basic science and engineering courses belonging to a discipline. These should be awarded during first and second years of the program. Each micro-project may have credit value equal to 0.25 to 0.50.

The **minor –projects** are problem solving experiences having 0.5 to 2 credit value which cut across 5 to 8 Engineering courses and one or two interdisciplinary engineering courses. These are awarded during middle period of an engineering program.

The **major projects** are open ended complex engineering problem solving or designing experiences which have value ranging from 6 to 10 credits. These experiences should give an opportunities to apply most of courses of a discipline along with a number of interdisciplinary considerations of engineering concepts and laws. Major projects can be split into two parts first part may be called as **pre-major project** which should be given in the pre-final semester and the second part as major project which should be awarded in the final semester.

There are a few **weaknesses or concerns in the system** which should be taken care of before making any innovation in the project method of learning-teaching.

1. Each & **every faculty guide** should be competent enough to execute a R&D project work at a higher level of any major projects undertaken by graduates of the department.

2. Each and **every faculty guide** with more than 3 years of experience teaching & or industrial job should be oriented with participative project method where continuous monitoring of progress of projects undertaken is planned and recorded as per mutually agreed upon schedules.

3. The **selection of project titles** and the members of project team should be decided by mutual consultation between faculty guide and the team members. Students should never be left on their own for searching and finalizing project titles and team members as they are too immature & in-experienced in understanding the real contributions of experiences of project work on their POs and employability skills.

   a. The collection of project titles should be an on-going process to which every stake holder can and should contribute. When students take industrial training, their one of the tasks should be to collect challenging real industry oriented problem which can be converted into students' major project problems.

    b.   The students should register for project one semester in advance with three alternative project titles along with suggested team members. The department should facilitate the team to finalize the project title within a period of 3 to 4 weeks.

    c.   They should complete the pre-major project in the remaining period of the pre-final semester along with synapsis of major project, technical paper on justification of the project title and their plan for solving the problem etc.

4.   The department should prepare an interactive website for organizing all such academic activities related to high order learning methods. Department should maintain all necessary records till the students get worthwhile employment.

5.   Every student should be ***discouraged** to purchase **'project appliance and its report'*** from the project shops opened in every major cities of developing countries to help incompetent students somehow complete the requirements of the engineering program by investing their parents money in an unethical transaction. Such practice goes completely against all professional ethics and responsibilities of graduates towards the community they hail from and they are likely to serve in future.

The method of 'project work experiences' can be divided in to the following five stages. These stages and responsibilities of student team members during each of these stages should be explained clearly.

    i.   Identify, understand and **specify the problem** and its boundary conditions. Describe targets, resources and constraints. Every student must be asked to maintain the logbook of project work right from the first day of award of the project work.

    ii.   Develop **optional solutions** and describe salient features each potential solution briefly.

    iii.   Select **one solution** which the project team wishes to pursue with sufficient justifications. Present the solution to peers and receive feedback for modifications.

    iv.   **Implement the solution**, test the prototype output and prepare a draft report, discuss the report with the project guide and receive feedback.

v. Make final presentation to peers, share learning outcomes and submit the **project report** along with the output of the project work to the department.

3.6: INNOVATIONS IN STUDENTS' ASSESSMENT

Students come to the college for learning entry professional competence and getting certification of their abilities on the bases of their evaluation using different modes of measurement and assessment of their performance. In outcome based system, certification need to be done both by the affiliating university and the college depending upon the POs of the program.

In education, assessment is the process of measuring and documenting, students'; level of knowledge, skills, attitudes and beliefs. Assessments allow educators to know in concrete terms how effective their learning-teaching has been. It is the evidence that learning has occurred.

Assessments can have a motivational effect on student achievement. Students who receive either praise and encouragement or correction are more motivated to improve their performance. Teachers who use assessment tools are more effective in reaching those students who are struggling. By using a variety of assessment tools, teachers can help all students succeed. They can avoid conflicts with students and guardians over the fairness of grades if they have a documented record of prior assessments in the students' portfolio to refer to during meetings with guardians. Pre-tests gauge students' level of prior knowledge of a course- cluster. Viva or Verbal questioning during the presentation of the material measures their comprehension. Written responses to their classwork guide them deeper into the material. A summative project work of some other performance based assignment gives a chance to show mastery of a course or skill. Some basic & important terms related to examination process are;

Measurement: Measurement is concerned with assigning a number, numerical quantity or giving a quantitative description (grade) to a certain characteristic/, ability or trait of a student. This numerical quantity or description is also called a test score or marks or grade awarded, if a test is given for measurement.

Assessment: In comparison to measurement, assessment, however, is concerned with determining the worth of something. This can be done by quantitative and/or qualitative descriptions or grade plus some value judgments. Thus we see that it has a value aspect added in judging the worth. In the educational context, a student's achievement on a certain course can be assessed - where it includes examining, marking/grading, certifying and so on. Assessment is, thus, more than measurement.

Evaluation: The term evaluation on the other hand has been used in a wider context; though retaining the concept of determining the worth of something. Normally it has been associated with the programs, projects, and institutions, like evaluation of program, evaluation of project, instructional evaluation or evaluation of a department or institution.

The types of assessment:

- Terminal or Summative assessment
- Formative or Continuous assessment

Terminal assessment measures the total effect of learning during a semester, ranks the quantum of learning by different students. Unit tests, Mid-term tests and Semester end Tests are examples of Summative assessment. The most important reforms in the terminal assessment is encouraging a high quality innovative, more objective, and short answer based question papers both in the internal & external question papers. Second most critical quality improvement shall be resulted by reducing the time gap between the tests and announcement of its results.

Formative or Continuous assessment helps in measuring the progress of learning during the formation of learning and may be performed by two approaches. In outcome based education system, development of continuous assessment system in tune with the POs presents the most challenging and interesting innovation for quality assurance. Continuous assessment records can be used to certify many competences manifesting the implications of attitudinal abilities. The continuous assessment shall two types of assessment instruments;

i. **Direct assessment instruments** in which the directly observable & measurable parameters are used to quantify the quality of performance.

ii. **Indirect assessment instruments** observes effects in behavior and trends in decision making or preferences in choices which are caused by some **value** being formed in a student. Such cause and effect relationships are used in designing a variety of assessment rubrics.system with the total set of concepts of Mission, PEOs, POs etc, with the performance indicators used in formulating assessment instruments.

There are a few more terms which should be thoroughly understood before developing any assessment system for students' learning as well as planning any reform in the assessment system.

- Validity
- Reliability
- Precision

Validity: When evaluation instruments are capable of measuring the parameters compatible/ identical to the desired aspects to be evaluated then the evaluation process is termed as valid process. Suppose pressure inside the tire of a wheel of a car is to be measured, if the instrument suitable for measuring pressure with appropriate range of scale is used, then the measurement will result into a **"valid pressure measuring"** process

In technical education context, use of viva-voce for measuring the experimental skills acquired by students through lab work, cannot be said as a valid process. However, if the goal is to assess the pre-requisite knowledge and interactive skills related to experimental skills, then the viva voce may become a valid evaluation process.

Reliability: Reliability indicates reproducibility of result of evaluation comparable within a tolerance zone.

If a hockey player is practicing for reliable goal producing skills, and he is putting the football between two target goal posts, then he can be treated as a reliable goal scorer.

Figure 3.1, shows the total process of aligning the assessment of PEOs and POs

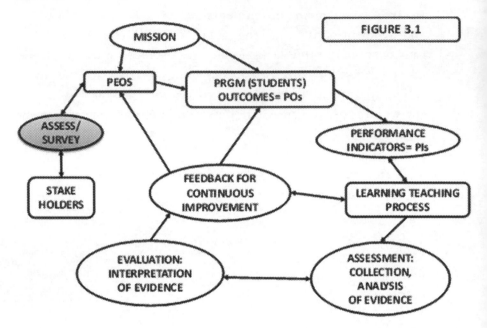

FIGURE 3.1

In technical education if a paper pencil test has be used over a group of students who so ever be examiner, the performance of individual students and their rank order is comparable, then the "paper-pencil test" will prove to be "reliable" evaluation/ assessment process.

Precision: Precision indicates the "tightness of tolerance" or tighter range of variability of a reliable process. If a player every time puts ball very close to target point between the two posts, he is reliable as well as precise and he cannot be defeated easily by the goal keeper. In educational context, short answer test paper shall be more precise than an essay type test paper. If answers of a short answer question are to the point, then most of the examiners shall award comparable marks within a tighter range.

Quality Assurance Reforms in Assessment:

- Reform internal assessment into a real continuous assessment of students' performance. Declare the criteria of internal assessment to increase transparency and objectivity.

- Unit Tests & Mid-term tests should have adequate well drafted objective and short answer questions as per specifications of test papers commensurate with the requirements of certifying POs and monitoring PEOs.
- Try to influence paper setters of the university to improve quality of university examination papers.
- Declare the test results as early as possible. Orient students not to repeat the common mistakes they have committed in the tests.
- Develop computing formats & software for making smart entries & collation of marks/ grades. This shall enable in declaring results at an early date.

3.7: INNOVATIONS IN INDUSTRY- INSTITUTE PARTNERSHIP

Many professional institutions do not care much about this aspect. They do some meetings, write informal letter to industry through the trainee students to help students during visits and training phase etc. and think there role is over. This area requires more attention and investment of time of the departments to improve the employability of both faculty and graduates. The relationship with industry should be beyond interactions till we achieve partnership with industry.

The partnership should benefit both the partner parties. A few example shall clarify the directions of reforms if some of the following benefits are not realized at your end.

Benefits to Industry

- Orientation & Training of practicing engineers and technologists in to emerging products, processes and technologies
- Training of practicing engineers in new management concepts & practices,
- Acquiring skills in doing action research, analyses of data and writing/ presenting reports. Publishing joint research papers in magazines.
- Off-loading simpler problem -solving to faculty and students teams of the institution and solving long-term problems at much lower costs. Patenting researched technologies jointly.

- Possibility of selecting more suitable graduates on the bases of the past interactions during their industrial visits and training.

Benefits to Institution

- Placement of students for visits and training in industry. Some of the graduates may also get jobs.
- Getting ideas of simpler industrial problems which help in designing micro, minor and major students' projects and designing assignments.
- Getting recognition of institution's better educational performance by acquiring accreditation from industries as well as from regulatory bodies. Thus enhancing the brand value of the institution.
- Orientation of faculty & students in the current needs of the industry.
- Contributions of industrial experts in teaching learning of topics & assignments which shall enhance employability skills.

Transforming the T&P function into a full Finishing schools function should be the aim of quality assurance reform in to this particular aspect of the institution.

3.8: FINISHING SCHOOL AND PLACEMENT CENTER

1. POs represent the entry level employability competence of the graduates. Many attitudinal personality attributes or competence are developed by observations of observing behavior of professionals in industrial environment. So the students, when proceed for industrial visits or training, should be properly oriented by the Professor (T&P) regarding the following points;

  - Why visit /training? What are the aims and objectives of visit or training?
  - What to observe and learn?
  - Who are the professional with whom to discuss the problems & solutions?

- What shall be reported after training/visit? Reports & presentations to continuously develop their communication skills.
- Which kind of problems are to be studied and undertaken to solve through project work? & so on.

If the students are properly oriented before starting of training or visit the effectiveness of learning shall improve by substantial degrees.

2. There are many students who might face individual learning problems. Such students should be tutored by organizing extra classes and practical work right from the 2nd Semester onwards. These experiences of counselling, extra coaching & practical work shall help in developing POs and accomplishing PEOs over the remaining semesters of the program.

3. Development of entrepreneurship in the graduates is an important function of the Finishing school. It should be integrated with the existing T&P section of the institute.

4. The finishing school should also try to forward to the departments, the marks or grades acquired by individual students as indicators of their acquisition of POs and contribute in continuous assessment and keeping its records.

5. The existing section of T&P should be expanded by adding faculty members of communications skills and social sciences, if any.

3.9: R&D, ENTREPRENEURSHIP AND CONSULTANCY CENTER

The faculty members need to realize that if their expertise is not being valued by their community, then they are not fulfilling their obligation of contributing to the economy of the country. If the industry and commerce trust on the capability of the faculty and the department of the Engg. Institution, then they should consult the department for finding out possible solutions of their problems. If the department starts receiving problems from the surrounding community, then automatically some of the following benefits will be accomplished by the institution;

- Enhanced problem solving skills in the faculty members which shall percolate to students with time ensuring improved quality of confidence and learning by students.
- Students also get part time sundry jobs in assisting faculty in conduction of research and creation of sundry jobs for students in providing assistance in research work.
- Many good ideas for formulating micro, minor and major projects shall be generated while working on research and open ended problem solving projects. Thus Poor & needy students shall find part-time small jobs in the R&D projects along with rich problem solving experiences.
- Extra revenue shall be generated by the institute which shall encourage a lot of action research and development as well as motivation to experts to join the institution.
- More financial assistance shall come from Governments' development funds for improving quality of education.
- Many faculty shall register for PhD dissertation work due to quality research facilities in the department.
- Higher brand value of the institution.

Foreign students would like to join the institution and faculty retention shall improve without extra efforts and investment.

CHAPTER 4.0

CURRICULUM MODIFICATIONS (TO ACCOMPLISH POS & PEOS)

4.1: Accreditation Criteria of NBA India & surrounding countries
4.2: Innovations for Quality Improvement in curriculum implementation
4.3: Modifying Curriculum of University
4.4: Evaluation and Assessment Rubrics

4.1: ACCREDITATION CRITERIA OF NBA, INDIA

National Board of Accreditation (NBA) is an autonomous regulatory agency for accreditation of professional programs under the ministry of human resources development of Govt. of India. NBA represents India as full signatory member of Washington Accord. NBA has adopted accreditation criteria from the Washington Accord for UG Engineering and Technology programs. NBA's accreditation related guidelines and formats have been finalized in Jan 2013. Currently (2014) Graduates of Accredited Technical Programs from India and neighboring countries like Sri Lanka and Singapore can move smoothly in any one of the 17 signatory countries and find jobs, join further education and seek licensees to practice as chartered Engineers. The students of any other country shall also get attracted to India and signatory countries provided they maintain truly high levels of quality of the professional education services in the universities and colleges.

The criteria, similar to those of B.E./ B. Tech. programs, have been used for both Diploma and PG programs in Engg & Technology. NBA, India have differentiated the two types of institutions on the basis of the degree of academic autonomy for modifying curriculum of the program to be accredited.

A- Accreditation of T-I class of institutions: It is meant for Autonomous & Government and Government aided institutions or University Institute of Technology (UIT). Criteria of T-I Accreditation has more weight on assessing outcome based educational criteria as compared to programs belonging to Class T-II institutions. These institutions can modify their curriculum with ease as they are the part of the university with adequate autonomy.

Accreditation certification is awarded when total score of marks of the program is between 600 and 750 with minimum qualifying marks as specified in the SAR document and accreditation manual.

B- Accreditation of T-I class of institutions: It is meant for non-autonomous Govt., self-financing and Govt.-aided institutions. Such institutions offer programs whose curriculum is designed by the affiliating or regulating external affiliating universities or Boards of examinations. It gives more weight on assessing input & output based criteria. ***These institutions can modify curriculum only by teaching extra topics & training in additional abilities.***

A program seeking accreditation under TIER-II should score a minimum of 750 points in aggregate out of 1000 points with minimum score of 60% in mandatory fields as specified in the SAR document and accreditation manual.

NBA's Accreditation manual (Jan 2013) provides the following criteria for certifying accreditation of the ***Bachelor of Engg programs.***

A: Criteria for BE Programs (10+2+4 years): version Jan, 2013

#	Criteria Institution's of class	Max & Min Marks for	
		T-I	T-II
1.	Vision, Mission & PEOs	100 & 60	75 & 45
2.	Program Outcomes	225 & 135	150 & 90
3.	Program Curriculum	125 & 75	125 & 75
4.	Students' Performance in the Program	75 & 45	100 & 60
5.	Faculty Contributions	175 & 105	175 & 105
6.	Facilities and Technical Support	75 & 45	125 & 75
7.	Academic Support & Teaching Learning Processes	75 & 45	75 & 45
8.	Governance, Institutional Support and Financial Resources	75 & 45	75 & 45
9.	Continuous Improvement	75 & 45	100 &60
	Total	1000 & 600	

B: Criteria for Diploma Engg Programs (10 +3 years): version Jan, 2013

#	Criteria or Institutions of class	Max & Min Marks f	
		T-I	T-II
1.	Vision, Mission & PEOs	75 & 45	75 & 45
2.	Program Outcomes	225 & 135	200 & 120
3.	Program Curriculum	100 & 60	100 & 60
4.	Students' Performance in the Program	100 & 60	100 & 60
5.	Faculty Contributions	100 & 60	100 & 60
6.	Facilities and Technical Support	100 & 60	100 & 60
7.	Academic Support & T-L Processes	150 & 90	150 & 90
8.	Governance, Institutional Support and Financial Resources	75 & 45	100 & 60
9.	Continuous Improvements	75 & 45	100 & 60
	Total	1000 & 600	

Please note that in case of BE programs, the accreditation criteria give more weight on the criteria 1, 2 & 3 for the programs offered by autonomous institutions as compared to those of programs of non-autonomous institutions. The enhanced weights are compensated by increasing weights of criteria 4, 6 and 9 as is obvious above.

4.2: QUALITY IMPROVEMENT IN CURRICULUM IMPLEMENTATION

All India Council of Technical Education have used a modified model of curriculum development to suite the requirements of outcome based technical education. The traditional deemed to be Universities, State & Central Universities and Technical Universities who have autonomy of designing curriculum of their affiliated Technical Colleges, do use an entirely different and simplistic course based curriculum model. This situation is responsible in making accreditation process of such course based programs more complex and difficult.

It is suggested that the colleges who are offering traditional 'courses based B.E. or Diploma Engineering programs' should try to understand the structure of the AICTE's latest Model Curricula and the kinds of learning-teaching experiences it intends to impart to the graduates of BE and DE programs. They should also undertake deep analyses of AICTE's curriculum and try to modify their own syllabi for initiating the implementation of outcome based technical education system. This kind of analysis and efforts of planning for implementation of their traditional syllabi shall help them understand the requirements of accreditation criteria of outcome based technical education system.

This process shall minimize their conceptual difficulties in preparing documentation for NBA's UGC's accreditation or any other international accreditation like ABET or IAO.

NAAC-UGC, India: Accreditation Criteria (www.*ugc*.ac.in*)*

I.	Curricular Aspects	*(Input + Process)*
II.	Teaching-Learning and Evaluation	*(Process)*
III.	Research, Consultancy and Extension	*(Input + Process)*

IV.	Infrastructure and Learning Resources	*(Input)*
V.	Student Support and Progression	*(Input + Process)*
VI.	Governance and Leadership	*(Input + Process)*
VII.	Innovative Practices	*(Input + Process+ output)*

ABET, USA: Criteria for Accrediting Engineering Programs 2014 - 2015
(http://www.abet.org/eac-criteria-2014-2015/#sthash.WmUThy1Q.dpuf)

1.	Students	*(Input)*
2.	Program Educational Objectives (PEOs)	*(Outcome)*
3.	Student Outcomes (SOs or POs)	*(Outcome)*
4.	Continuous Improvement	*(Input +Process + output+ outcome)*
5.	Curriculum	*(Input+ Process)*
6.	Faculty	*(Input)*
7.	Facilities	*(Input + Process)*
8.	Institutional Support	*(Input)*

IAO's criteria for accreditation (www.iao.org)

1.	Academics	*(Input+ Process + output)*
2.	Faculty	*(Input)*
3.	Facilities	*(Input+ Process)*
4.	Students	*(Input)*
5.	Financial Assistance	*(Input+ Process)*
6.	Demand in the Job Market	*(Outcome)*
7.	Foreign Students	*(Input)*
8.	Scholarships	*(Input+ Process)*
9.	Number of Programs	*(Input+ Process)*

It is obvious that only the criteria of NBA, India and ABET, USA require the program to specify the outcomes of the programs in terms of Program/ Student (learning) Outcome or POs / SOs and Program Educational Objectives or PEOs in addition to the criteria related to the inputs / infrastructure and educational processes. The UGC & IAO's criteria are related to the accreditation of the institution rather than the program and they do not require the statements of POs & PEOs related to individual programs offered by the institution. However, in case of IAO 'demand in job market' indicates indirectly the outcomes of the educational programs and the whole institution.

The current course based syllabi has oriented the foci of faculty members to the myth that the students somehow score good percentages of marks or higher grades in the university examinations of different courses constituting a graduation program. The faculty seldom think beyond students' achievements in the university examinations. It is therefore, when NBA had introduced outcome based accreditation system, they find difficult to formulate outcomes in terms of statements like PEOs & POs. In the following paragraphs, ideas have been shared to explain the tips & logic behind possible modifications in the existing syllabi & curricula so that the implementation of outcome based technical education can be initiated just after submission of application for accreditation.

4.3: MODIFYING CURRICULUM OF AFFILIATING UNIVERSITY

All India Council of Technical Education, MHRD, India (www.aicte-india.org) has developed during 2011-13, 'Model syllabi for Bachelor of Engineering' for disciplines of Agriculture Engg., Pharmacy, Engineering & Technology, Hotel Management & Catering Technology and Architecture. In the syllabi pertaining to Engg. & Technology, the courses have been included which fall one of the following course clusters.

a. Humanities & Social Science (HS)
b. Basic Science (BS)
c. Engg Science (ES)
d. Professional Core (PC)
e. Professional Electives (PE)
f. Open Electives (OE)
g. Project & Training (PT)
h. Mandatory Course (MC)

Mandatory Courses: Course work on peripheral subjects in a program, wherein familiarity considered mandatory; To be included as non-Credit,

Mandatory Courses, with only a pass in each required to qualify for Degree award from the concerned institution; Such Courses to be limited to < 5 % of the maximum permissible Course/Credit Load;

Many GAs & POs are supplemented and supported by the subject matter included in the new clusters such as Humanities and Social Sciences, Open Electives and Mandatory Courses. Naturally such topics are not found in the traditional syllabi of most of the affiliating universities

The following are two examples of curricula analyses; one curricula of Electronics and Communication Engineering belonging to Rajiv Gandhi Technical University, Bhopal, M.P., India and the other one pertains to model syllabi of AICTE, MHRD, India. You can appreciate the difference in the two syllabi as far as their suitability to facilitate development of abilities implied in graduate attributes of Washington accord or NBA, India.

When you compare the % credits given to a particular course cluster by your affiliating university with the range of % recommended by AICTE's model curriculum development approach, then you can appreciate the modifications desired in the content of the syllabi you are required to teach. The modifications in syllabi can only be done by adding some more topics & assignment to compensate the existing deficiencies in the syllabi.

The model syllabi have been developed by AICTE, India keeping the following aspects which are quite compatible to the curricular requirements of the Washington accord. The aspects considered while designing model syllabi of BE program in Electronics and Communication Engineering are given below.

T-4.1: Curriculum Analysis-1: BE Electronic & Communications RGPV, Bhopal, MP, India

Course Clusters	Title	RGPV Curriculum Credits					AICTE's Range of % of Credits	
		L Hrs 1=1cr	T Hrs 1=0.5 cr	P Hrs 1=0.5 cr	Sub-total Credits	% Credit	Min	Max
HS	Humanities & Social Science	6	2	19	17.5	10.08	5	10
BS	Basic Science	15	5	4	19.5	11.23	15	20

ES	Engineering Science	18	6	17	29.5	17.00	15	20
PC	Professional Core	69	40	19	88.5	**51	30	40
PE	Professional Electives	9	3	0	10.5	*6.05	10	15
OE	Open Electives	0	0	0	0	0	5	10
PT	Project	0	0	16	8	*4.61	10	15
MC	Mandatory Course	0	0	0	173.5	0		8 units
	Total Hrs	117	56	248	173.5	-	-	
	Credits	117	28	37.5	173.5	100%		
*	Needs enhancement of credits of course contents							
**	Needs reduction of credits of course contents							

AICTE's approach to Curriculum Development of BE in Electronics and Communications (EC): (www.aicte-india.org)

As a major objective of *E&T* education in India now is to develop *E&T* professionals having competencies, intellectual skills and knowledge equipping them to contribute to the society through productive and satisfying careers as *innovators, decision makers and leaders* in the national and global economies of the 21st century, the *Approach to Curriculum* for *UG E&T Degree Programs* needs to lay special emphasis on educating/preparing the students well for being able to demonstrate the following abilities:

(a) Effective application of *knowledge* of mathematics, science and technical subjects;
(b) Planning and design to conduct scientific and technical experiments;
(c) Analysis and interpretation of scientific, technical and economic data collected;
(d) Design of parts, subsystems, systems and/or processes to meet specific needs;
(e) Identification, formulation and solving of problems using simulation or otherwise;

(f) Use of techniques/tools including software in all disciplines, as may be required;

(g) Effective communication skills and leadership/participation in team work;

(h) Fulfillment of professional, social and ethical responsibilities;

(i) Sensitivity to environmental and energy issues and concerns;

(j) Planning, development and implementation of strategies for life-long learning.

Please note the aspects considered in the design and development of AICTE's model syllabi have been derived from the Graduate Attributes recommended in the Washington Accord. These are the attributes on the basis of which the POs or program outcomes are formulated any Graduate technology program.

The analyses of AICTE's curriculum for BE in EC reveals its structure and allocation of credits to different course clusters as described below in table 4.2.;

Structure of presenting a course

AICTE has suggested a structure for presenting a course content which shall become clear by going through the following sample structure.

1. Department: Electronics & Communication
2. Course Code: BE (EC-304)
3. Title of Course: BACHELOR OF ENGINEERING
4. Course Cluster: HS/BS/ES/PC/PE/P&T/Extra Curricular: *PC*
5. Status of Course: Compulsory or elective: Comp.
6. Type of Course: Theory/Lab/Project/Training/
   Others (Please Tick):   *Theory and Lab*
7. Code Numbers of Prerequisite course: *BE-104 BEEE and BE-201 Engg. Physics*
8. Topics in different units
9. References for further studies: Books, journals, websites etc.
10. Academic Eligibility of Faculty members 1- the one who is proposing modifications & 2 –the other who is editing & validating the modifications.

T-4.2: Curriculum Analysis-2: Model syllabi of Electronics and communications (AICTE version-Oct., 2012)

Course Cluster	Title	# of Courses	Theory Credits (L+T+P)	% of credits	AICTE's recommended Range of credit %	
					Min %	Max %
HS	Humanities & Social Sciences	5	18	8.91	5	10
BS	Basic Sciences	16	38	18.81	15	20
ES	Engineering Sciences	12	43	21.28	15	20
PC	Professional Core	21	53	26.23	30	40
PE	Professional Electives	6	18	8.91	10	15
PW	Project work	0	20	9.9	10	15
OE	Open Electives	4	12	5.36	5	10
MC	Mandatory Courses	6	0	0.00	0	0
	Total	70	202	100.00		

11. Contact Hours   L:T:P::3:1:2
      Total Hours-6   Credits-4.5
        (Two hours of T & P = 1 credit)

12. Course Outcomes:
    a. Students acquire basic the knowledge about Electronic circuit and Devices like BJT, FET, UJT etc.
    b. Students understand the process of achieving high speed Switching.

13. Course Contents Unit -1 to 5
{Topics and practical work added in different units of existing syllabus.} Note-indicate in separate snake brackets.

Steps in Curriculum Modifications by Non-autonomous Institutions

(a) On similar lines explained above you can compare syllabi which has been framed by your affiliating university with any other syllabi framed for outcome based technical education and make the bare minimum modifications by adding topics and assignments/ experiments & project work etc.

(b) The institute should think of constituting a Departmental Advisory Board whose members should represent the stakeholders such as Alumni to take care of students' interests, Industry & commerce, faculty and management, entrepreneurs, regulatory bodies and the experts of the discipline. The advisory board's primary function should be to validate the proposed curriculum modifications and monitoring its proper implementation.

(c) It is assumed that the department shall keep in touch with the continuous changes occurring in the job market and arrange for theoretical and practical inputs to students from experienced professional stake holders to make them aware of the future they are going to confront as well as how to prepare for facing future challenges.

(d) Conduct one day search conference or seminars with participation of critical stake holders and collect current trends in the job market as well as get their feedback on your planned and executed academic activities for improving the services in future.

(e) Modify the assessment system for judging the progress & performance of students in the courses and all other activities encouraged by the institute. Outcome based system of education requires a variety of assessment strategies and focus on continuous assessment as compared to what attention we are paying to summative assessment. Assessment of attitudinal or behavioral abilities is quite complex and cannot be assessed simply by those instruments which are being used traditionally for summative or terminal assessment. We need to design instruments which can take care of both quantitative and qualitative criteria for measuring the degree of successful performance of students continuously and providing the corrective feedback to students as soon as possible.

Let us try to understand about assessment rubrics which shall form an important item of overall quality improvement of educational services.

4.4: RUBRICS FOR EVALUATION AND ASSESSMENT

Evaluation tools and instruments can be classified in to two simple classes

- Direct Evaluation and
- Indirect Evaluation

Direct evaluation is done by processes of reading or observing the written response or visual performance of students during continuous and terminal assessment or observing students presentations or oral answers etc.

Indirect evaluation is done by surveying for opinions and collecting information from others those who have been observing students performing or interacting with them on some unconnected issues to judge their personality attributes and indications of attitudes. Some of the examples of indirect evaluation are given below;

Alumni Survey: Collection of a wide variety of information about program satisfaction, how well students are prepared for their careers, what types of jobs or graduate degrees majors have gone on to obtain, and the skills that are needed to succeed in the job market or in graduate study, 3 years after the graduation. Provide the information opportunity to collect data on which areas of the program should be changed, altered, improved or expanded.

Employer Survey: Provide information about the curriculum, Survey programs and course outcomes, on-the-job-field- specific information about the application and value of the skills that the program offers. It helps to determine if their graduates have the necessary job skills and if there are other skills that employers particularly value that graduates are not acquiring in the program.

Student Exit: To evaluate the success of the program in survey providing students with opportunities to achieve the program outcomes.

Course Exit: To determine the quality of the course, the Survey various outcomes, that this course tries to satisfy, and the level of achievement of these outcomes.

Project evaluation: This is a demonstration of the abilities of an evaluation of student throughout the program.

Course evaluation: It gives information about what and how evaluation students are learning within the classroom environment, using existing information that faculty routinely collect by test / end-semester exam performance, assignments etc., and other methods of assessing student learning within the classroom environment.

Guidelines for selecting assessment methods

- The evidence you collect depends on the questions you want to answer. The sample questions for the program assessment are

  - o Does the program meet or exceed certain standards?
  - o How does the program compare to others?
  - o Does the program do a good job at what it sets out to do?
  - o How can the program experience be improved?

- As many outcomes are difficult to assess using only one assessment tool, use multiple methods to assess each learning outcome.
- Include both direct and indirect measures.
- Include qualitative as well as quantitative measures.
- Choose assessment methods that allow you to assess the strengths and weaknesses of the program.

Assessment of PEOs

In case of Program educational objectives one should identify the indicators which indirectly indicate or illustrate features of successful achievement. For each indicator one can evolve a minimum success quantity in terms of % of goal or target assigned to indicate satisfactory success.

Assessment Rubrics: these are useful in assessment of POs

Rubric is a **set of performance indicators** which define and describe the **important components of task** being completed in line with the instructions of an assignment.

Rubric can be Generic or Task specific,

Generic Rubric:

- It can be used in case of performance of similar tasks,
- Big picture approach
- More subjectivity

Specific Task Rubric:

- Can only be used for a single specific task
- Focused approach
- More objective

Any rubric can be displayed in terms of a graphic representation or a tabular presentation of criteria and criteria value/ weight. An example of a tabular rubric shall illustrate the point.

Example 1: Specific Rubric-

Program Outcome or PO to be assessed is, 'Student can work effectively in Teams (Classroom seminar/ Library assignment)'

T-4.3: Example Specific Rubric or Rating scale

Criteria	Unsatis-factory D = 1	Deve-loping C = 2	Satis-factory B = 3	Exem-plary A = 4	Score Earned
Research & Gather info	Does not collect any information on the topic	Collects very limited info; some relate to the topic	Collects some basic info; most refer to the topic	Collects a great deal of information; all refer to the topic	
Full fill team's role & duties	Does not perform any duties assigned to team role	Performs very little duties	Performs nearly all duties	Performs all duties of assigned team role	

Share work equally	Always relies on others to do work	Rarely does the assigned work; needs reminding	Usually does the assigned work; rarely needs reminding	Always does the assigned work without any need to reminding
Listen to other team mates	Is always talking; never allows any to body to speak	Usually does most talking; rarely allows others to speak	Listens; but sometimes talk too much	Listens; speaks a fair amount

Note: Its outcome shall contribute to 35% of PO to be assessed

Example 2: SPECIFIC Rubric: for Lab work

XYZ Lab: BE Semester VI:

Relevant POs: Engg Knowledge, Develop Solutions, Investigate, Communicate & team work,

POs in specific Focus: Investigate & Communicate

T-4.4: Specific Rubric or Check-list for Lab work: Attainment of investigative & communication abilities

Abilities	Degree of attainment				Related Experiences
	D=30%	**C=50%**	**B=70%**	**A=80%**	
Conduct investigation	Fully guided	Partially guided	Hints based	Self-guided	For 3, 5, 8, Experi-ments
Effective written Communication	Partially copied report	Fairly original but traditional report	Fully original with fairly clear ideas	Original expression with innovative interpretation of event	2 & 4 Experi-ments
Effective oral Communication	Fumbling while speaking; no confidence	Speaking with lack of clarity; lack of confidence	Speak clearly but deficient listening; average confidence	Efficient listening and speaking with clarity & confidence	1, 6 & 7 Lab Demos

Example 3: Generic Rubric:

Program Outcome or PO: *'Design/Development solutions for a complex / inter-disciplinary Engg Problem'*,

Level- BE 4 years Program, Semester -VII

The Problems to be solved is, *'Develop an economical Desert Cooler to minimize the consumption of water and electric power and maintain comfort cooling in the climate of Chennai, India.'*

The problem solving team shall comprise of 2 students each from disciplines of ME, CE, EC, CSE & EX = total 10 students

T-4.5: GENERIC Tabular Rubric or Rating Scale

Criteria	Unsatis-factory D=1	Deve-loping C=2	Satis-factory B=3	Exem-plary A=4	Score Out of 10
Consult and elect a leader	Does take any interest and remains self-centered	Takes some interest in consultation, but avoids any possible hard work	Proposes his own name with a feeling doing less work	Proposes name of a person & justifies why?	
Leads in Analysis of Problem to break it into parts & task assignment	Asks every other person to explain the problem without any thinking	First tries to think it over and starts discussions without much planning	Asks for some time to think over and asks everybody to get prepared for discussion after a day	researches, works out a rough analysis & task allocation, circulates to members before discussions	
Research, Gather info & maintain a log book	Does not collect any information on the topic	Collects very limited info; some relate to the topic	Collects some basic info; most refer to the topic	Collects a great deal of information; all refer to the topic	

Full fill team's role & duties	Does not perform any duties assigned to team role	Performs very little duties	Performs nearly all duties	Performs all duties of assigned team role	
Share work equally	Always relies on others to do work	Rarely does the assigned work; needs reminding	Usually does the assigned work; rarely needs reminding	Always does the assigned work without any need to reminding	
Listen to other team mates	Is always talking; never allows any to body to speak	Usually does most talking; rarely allows others to speak	Listens; but sometimes talk too much	Listens; speaks a fair amount	
*Leader Presents the analysis	Presents orally without any visual support: CB / PPP/; Paper; avoids questions	Presents on Chalk Board with some rough scribbling on paper; Takes up only two questions	Presents on a white board with color markers with a supporting notes; invites limited 4 to 5 questions	Presents on a carefully prepared PPP and a supporting note; provokes questions and confidently satisfies all queries	

Thus for each PO or PEO there shall be number of indicators manifesting in the academic activities inside classrooms, tutorial room, laboratory and project work and during outdoor activities like sports, social services, army training, personality development assignments etc.

There shall be a requirement of designing a number of creative collation tables where all grades and marks awarded to students as a result of their written or oral responses and observations of their performances in different learning spaces shall be compiled and collated. The records of such collation tables need to be preserved carefully for formulating final assessment of different POs at the end of four or six or eight semesters of graduation program.

Thus, the total evaluation of abilities of the graduate during the final month shall be comprising of the following evaluation based certifications.

1. **Internal Institutional Certification**
   a. Marks or grades of courses based on continuous assessment during each semester
   b. Marks or grades against each PO indicating the attributes of entry level professional personality which shall illustrate first part of employability attributes of the graduate.

2. **External University Certification**
   a. Marks or grade sheets awarded showing the achievements in the university's summative evaluation in end of the semester theory and practical examinations which shall illustrate the second part of employability attributes of the graduate.
   b. The degree ensuring the international mobility as implied in the Washington or Dublin Accords.

CHAPTER 5.0

NBA ACCREDITATION OF UG PROGRAMS

5.1. NBA's- Approach to Accreditation Engg & Technology programs

5.2. Tips for creating a SAR: Criteria 1

5.3. Tips for creating a SAR: Criteria 2

5.4. Tips for creating a SAR: Criteria 3

5.5. Assessment Tools

5.6. Assessment Rubrics

5.1: NBA'S- APPROACH TO ACCREDITATION FOR ENGG & TECHNOLOGY PROGRAMS

The National Board of Accreditation (NBA) in its present form, as an independent organization, under the Societies Registration Act 1860 has come into existence with effect from 7th January, 2010, with the objective of assurance of quality and relevance of education, especially in technical disciplines through the mechanism of outcome based accreditation of programs and institutions offering technical and professional education (http://nbaind.org). NBA has invested a commendable & creative efforts and funds in developing documentations for guiding the process of accreditation of Engg and technology UG programs. They have developed a set of following documents for various disciplines of Engineering and Technology. This UG section includes two major disciplines of Engineering and Pharmacy.

- Set of **Tier-I** documents for Autonomous Institutions with power to change curriculum as per needs: Self-Assessment Report format (SAR), Manual & Evaluation report for some disciplines.
- Set of **Tier-II** documents for non-autonomous Institutes without power to change curriculum: Self-Assessment Report format (SAR), Manual & Evaluation report for some disciplines

The accreditation criteria of UG programs offered by two different levels of institutions are the same, only the weights allocated to some criteria in these two cases are slightly different considering the powers acquired by virtue of academic autonomy. The bold and italic fonts highlight those criteria where this difference has been made.

Criteria for BE Programs (10+2+4 years): version Jan, 2013

#	Criteria	Max & Min Marks for Institutions of class	
		T-I	T-II
1.	*Vision, Mission & PEOs*	*100 & 60*	*75 & 45*
2.	*Program Outcomes*	*225 & 135*	*150 & 90*
3.	Program Curriculum	125 & 75	125 & 75
4.	*Students' Performance in the Program*	*75 & 45*	*100 & 60*
5.	Faculty Contributions	175 & 105	175 & 105
6.	*Facilities and Technical Support*	*75 & 45*	*125 & 75*
7.	Academic Support & Teaching-Learning Processes	75 & 45	75 & 45
8.	Governance, Institutional Support and Financial Resources	75 &45	75 & 45
9.	*Continuous Improvement*	*75 & 45*	*100 &60*
	Total	1000 & 600	

NBA's approach is to give more weight or importance to criteria 1 & 2 (pertaining to Vision, mission and POs) to T-I institutes. These weights are compensated by increasing weights of other criteria # 4, 6 & 9 for T-II institutions. The logic for this differential treatment perhaps is based on the assumption that the criteria 4, 6 & 9 can be easily be controlled & complied with by non-autonomous institutions, whereas T-I institutions having power to change curriculum can easily comply with the requirements of criteria 1 & 2. The implementation of outcome based criteria of accreditation are more nearer to ideal situation in case of T-I institutions as compared to T-II institutions. This approach provides scope for professional institutions to make continuous improvements at a comparatively slower rate from T-II conditions to T-I conditions in step by step manner. This approach suits the circumstances of professional education sector prevailing in developing Asian & African countries. The approach of NBA commensurate with goals of Washington accord shall also introduce the outcome based technical education in technical institutions of India and surrounding countries.

5.2: TIPS FOR CREATING A SAR: CRITERIA 1

The Self-Assessment Report (SAR) is prepared by interested institutions for initiating application to NBA for accreditation visits of experts and awarding certificate of accreditation of a particular program in due course of time. The structure and its major contents of the SAR are explained below;

Structure of SAR

There are three parts in the SAR.

SAR-Part-I: it consists of Institutional, Departmental and specific program related information.

SAR-Part-II: it consists of information related to nine criteria mentioned earlier and their sub-sections with supporting questions and answers. At the end a formula is given for determining score of assessment of status of the institute against each sub-sections and overall assessment of the criteria. Some relevant portion of detailed SAR shall be illustrated later on.

SAR-Part-III: it comprises of two sets of 51 record files which should be compiled for inspection during the visits of the experts of NBA team. 17 files need to be prepared for collecting different specific records & evidences of achievements related to the institution. 32 files need to be compiled which are related to specific achievements and indicators of success related to a selected UG program. The detailed lists shall be given separately later on.

SAR-Part-II

In this section some critical portions of SAR shall be explained with the intension to facilitate those faculty members who may face typical conceptual difficulties while filling the SAR due to lack of experience in such aspects of the technical education.

Criteria-1: Vision, Mission and Program Educational Objectives (75 points)

1.1. **Vision and Mission** (5)

1.1.1. State the Mission and Vision of the institute and department (1)

State Vision of your Department & contribute to the vision of institute for a time period of next 10 years from the current academic year.
State Missions of department and those of the institute underpinning the following

- Remember that the vision defines the institution's aim including its educational activities, its student body, and its role within the education community. The institution's vision defines how well, and in what ways, it is accomplishing its goals and uses the results for broad-based, continuous planning and evaluation. Mission of the institute tells about the strategies of reaching the vision commensurate with observing the ethics and values of the owner & other stake holders of the institute. In other words, Mission statement defines what an institution is, why the institution exists, and its reason for being. It defines what we are here to do together.

- Focus on using strategies to assuring development of competencies in the graduates compatible to GAs of NBA (POs)
- Focus on futuristic global trends of employment market & scopes in higher studies for engineering graduates your program is aspiring to prepare (PEOs)
- Consider yours relevant SWOT, while thinking of strategies and time frame.

  o Maximize use of strength, have phased plans to overcome weaknesses,
  o Extract maximum benefits from the opportunities,
  o Plan aggressively to negotiate & avoid confrontation with threats in the initial years.

- Go through some of the good motivating statements of vision which inspire every stakeholder to contribute his/her best to excel.
- Be pragmatic! Because you have to comply with vision, mission and values in future.

Some of the lead questions those may be helpful in the creation of the Vision and Mission statements:

- What are the critical elements in our system?
- Who are the current stakeholders today – inside and outside?
- What are the most influential trends in our institution today?
- What aspects of our institution empower people?
- How is the strategic plan currently used?
- What major losses do we fear?
- What do we know (that we need to know)?
- Who are the stake holders of the institution?

1.1.2. Indicate how and where the Mission and Vision are published and disseminated (2)

- In the admission broacher of the department
- In the department section of the website

- On department notice & display Boards,
- In curriculum implementation documents for all the four years
- On the website section related to the program details
- In the laboratory manuals and laboratory charts/ posters
- On displays located on eye catching points of the department

1.1.3. Mention the process for defining the Mission and Vision of the department (2) The Process Steps:

I. **Conduct SWOT Analysis** of the department. SWOT stands for Strengths, Weaknesses, Opportunities and Threats.

    a) Develop a SWOT response format and collect responses from the representative sample stakeholders such as Senior-students, Parents, Alumni, Governors and managers, faculty members and technical staff. Approach as many alumni as possible and employers for giving their positive & negative impressions about the department and institute.

    b) Compile the responses and formulate the final SWOT of the Department.

II. **Arrive at Vision of the Department**

    a) Vision is your future you desire to create, described in present tense, as if it were happening now. It is where you aspire to reach and be like.

    b) Project the tentative SWOT of the Department and ask everybody to read it at-least two times

    c) Brain storm most of the faculty members of the department for their ideas of the future of the department say after five years in view of the SWOT of the Department.

    d) Head of Department should finalize the statement of Vision of the Department along with a few faculty & staff.

    e) The final Vision statement should be approved by the whole department and then workout mission on similar lines.

III. Arrive at Mission of the Department

   a) Mission elaborates reason why institute exists and wants to excel further through a variety of ways & means to reach the vision as soon as possible.
   b) Workout the mission statement in groups on similar lines for formulating vision as mentioned above.

1.2. Program Educational Objectives (15)

1.2.1. Describe the Program Educational Objectives (PEOs) (2)

   a. **PEOs:** Program Educational Objectives of the Dept. / program **indicate** the potential fields of employment & professional accomplishments within 3-4 years after graduation.
   b. Ideally PEOs are a set of about 5 to 6 statements manifesting what the dept./ program aims at for enabling graduates to accomplish in career positioning or in academics or in R&D, after 2 to 3 years of experience in the field of work or higher studies.

1.2.2. State how and where the PEOs are published and disseminated (2)
On similar lines as in 1.1.1

1.2.3. List the stakeholders of the program (1)

Final Year Students: Students have the maximum stake as they are investing time and efforts as well as risking their career in the hope of acquiring abilities & become an employable professional engineer after 4 years of studies in the college. Employability includes both self-employment and wage-employment.

Parents: Parents invest their hard earned money and risk the future of their wards with the college in the hope that all their investment shall return when their wards shall become an employable professional engineer and serve /support the family in future.

Employers: Industry and commerce: Although, they employ the candidates by a set of selection test, however, they have risk that the candidate may not perform to their satisfaction. Their investment of efforts

& funds in training and expenses on salaries may lead to losses if the candidates fail to perform as expected and may not contribute in the expected business growth of the employer & economy as a whole. Thus, the overall harmony and satisfaction level of the society depends upon the growth in economy.

Governors and Managers: Governors and managers share the risks and concerns of the investors in the establishment of the college. Professional Educational Services as a service sector enterprises need to earn profits and enhance its brand value continuously to attract better students and talented faculty and show growth of enterprise both qualitatively and quantitatively. Management's investment on operations of the college and efforts of faculty also goes to waste, if the graduate fails to perform. Sure return on investment in quality, needs tactful & strategic planning, execution and continual monitoring.

Faculty Members and staff: Faculty and staff after appointment need to learn continually on executing assigned tasks. Routine style of working does not impart rich experiences to faculty & graduates which the brand value of the both the parties does not improve. But when quality practices are pursued employees do face a lot of day to day challenges. Management needs to pay attention to such bottlenecks and help faculty in overcoming them.

Such an environment is generally liked by intelligent and dedicated faculty and staff. Overall employees' satisfaction level is generally higher in a quality conscious work environment. So quality practices attract talented faculty and staff and also promote their longer retention.

1.2.4. State the process for establishing the PEOs (5)

I.   Have comprehensive discussions on the outcome based technical education and relationships between the concepts of Vision, Mission, POs and PEOs with the senior faculty members of the department experienced in writing POs and PEOs.

II. Organize a search seminar in which stakeholders shall contribute their ideas related to the potential career options after 5 to 7 years in their respective disciplines and world of work.

III. Ask faculty members to explore and mine relevant information, number of examples of POs and PEOs. HoD, along with program co-coordinator faculty, shall draft PEOs in view of the findings of the search seminar, available examples of PEOs. Display PEOs through LCD projector for comments & feedback from the other faculty members and technical staff.

IV. HoD and two faculty members together shall draft the second version of the PEOs on the basis of the feedback received from the search seminar etc.

V. Discuss & semi-finalize Vision, Mission, PEOs and draft POs in the departmental meeting.

VI. *Department Advisory Board (DAB)* shall finally approve all the statements of Vision, mission, PEOs & draft POs. DAB shall continually monitor the accomplishment of PEOs and keep on reviewing the PEOs statements from time to time.

1.2.5. Establish consistency of PEOs with Mission of the institute (5)

Consistency between PEOs and Mission of the Program/ dept.

The correlation and consistency amongst the PROs and the missions of the department / institute should be checked by making a table with first column of PEOs, second column of parts of mission manifesting consistency with a PEO and the third column indicating the degree of consistency or correlation may be in terms of 3 grades. The grade A may mean high consistency, B for medium consistency and C may be used for low consistency. Prepare a 3 column table as shown below.

PEOs	Components of Missions	Degree of consistency

1.3. Achievement of program educational objectives (20)

1.3.1. Justify the academic factors involved in achievement of the PEOs (5)

Curricular Components:

I. Improved structure of the Curriculum of the program commensurate with AICTE's model curriculum:

    a. POs

    b. PEOs

    c. Description of Classification of Course Clusters & AICTE's Range of credits: HS=5-10%, BS=15-20%, ES=15-20%, PC= 30-40%, PE=10-15%, PT= 10-15%, Mandatory Courses = equivalent to about 5-8 hours/week?

    d. Credit allocations to L-T-P sessions and balancing % as per norms.

    e. Description of Outcomes of courses & Course-Clusters & correlation matrix with PEOs/ POs

    f. Encouraging use of Learning-teaching methods by Individual theory Courses:

        i.   Interactive Lecture with rich AV Aids and tutorial methods

        ii. Professional confidence, lifelong learning and communication & presentation skills by classroom seminars & library assignments

        iii. Group discussion on textual and video case-studies/ Library / Tutorial assignments.

        iv. Self-study using books, journals, A-V materials and web-surfing.

    g. Encouraging use of Learning-Teaching methods of Experiential Learning with a focus to achieve POs & PEOs:

        1. Team work & average problem solving through Labs & Micro projects,

        2. Skill development & housekeeping Workshops,

        5. Awareness of work culture by Industrial visits & skills enrichment by industrial Training,

        6. Team work and leadership training thru Complex problem solving through Minor and Major Projects,

7. Creative and competitive design problem-solutions & applying IT tools thru Competitive Technical Exhibitions (Robotics/ Working Models)

8. Applications IT tools by Competitive Software applications, simulations / animations clips, PPTs, Posters etc.

9. Creativity, Communications skills, socialization & team working /leadership thru Drama & fine arts exhibitions, Extempore Debates on instant themes & Debates on allocated themes, regional seminars etc., sports & games

10. Students' Competitive paper-presentations: in Professional Society's Inter-college – Conferences and debates, college sponsored competitions

11. Socialization and sensitivity to environment and people at large thru community service and participation in NCC & NSS.

h. Keeping secured records of continuous & terminal assessment of students' performances in their personal portfolios for both theory and experiential learning.

SIGNIFICANCES OF PEOS

• PEOs are meant to guide the program toward continual improvement.

• PEOs provide concrete and measurable steps toward achievement of goals. Also, they provide the crucial link between the program and the needs of stakeholders in the program and the Vision and Mission of the Department and the institution.

• The PEOs would be helpful in careful curriculum design, continual monitoring of students' progress, assessment of outcomes, and evaluation of the curriculum by the program.

• Primary and major stakeholders. Establishment of the PEOs normally follows the process of identification of stakeholder needs.

Achievement of PEOs has to be measured on the bases of different indicators (Quantities of indices) the following classes of activities undertaken by the department in order to achieve PEOs in the time frame of 3 to 4 years after graduation.

- **Quality Improvements** in Physical resources and infrastructures to improve practical training. *(Target indicator- 40% improvement in 1st year, 90% in second yr and 100% in 3rd yr.)*
- **Quality improvement** in the qualification, experiences, retention and contributions of faculty members *(Target indicator in faculty indices of 5 to 10% every year)*
- **Quality improvement** in admission cutoff and entry and exit abilities of students/ scholars *(admission cutoff improves by say 3 to 5 % every year)*
- **Quality improvement** in placement before or within period after graduation and career growth *(target indicator achieved 75% for 1st batch, 90% for 2nd batch and 95% for 3rd batch)* and noticeable accomplishments in targeted areas and career growth after 3 to 4 years after graduations *(target indicator achieved 75% for 1st batch, 85% for 2nd batch and 90% for 3rd batch).*

1.3.2. Explain how the administrative system helps in ensuring the achievement of the PEOs (5)

Structural improvements at Institute Level

a. **Board of Governors and its regulations**. It governs the system and provide policy level guidance and necessary support to director by delegating managerial/ administrative powers for implementing its orders and decisions. It should meet at least three to four times every year and formulate quality facilitating policies and regulations.

b. **Internal Quality Assurance Committee (IQAC) and regulatory functions:** it should consists of members who shall represent HoDs, External expert faculty, representatives of Director of Tech Education (DTE) and University, Director as Chairman and Senior HoD as secretary of the council. It shall validate all proposals of Institute level policies and regulations common to all the depts. it should meet at least once in a semester

c. **Finishing School (FS):** The office of TPO plus communication skills faculty are transformed in to Finishing School: It takes care of all activities of Personality Development for Employability, Industrial

Training of students, and Campus Based placement of graduates. It is also responsible to arrange for effective communication of the concerns of employers to the concerned Departments and faculty so that employability can be improved. It shall conduct all kinds of opinion surveys and organize Alumni meets etc.

Structural improvements at Department Level

a. **Department Advisory Boards (DAB) and its regulatory function:** it should comprise of faculty members internal as well as external if possible, HoD as Secretary of the board. Validates all academic matters related to the Dept. Meets two times in a semester. It should form a communication bridge between faculty members and the management.

b. **Program Assessment Committee** and its functions: Its chairperson should be HoD and Program coordinator as secretary to tackle all the issues related to assessment of students. It keeps records of continuous improvements, update all relevant records & websites, policies regulations related to internal continuous assessment and University terminal Evaluation.

c. **Program Coordinator:** This person is academic head of the group of program faculty and is responsible for planning, implementation and evaluation of the degree of success of the program. S/he shall be responsible for preparing SAR on behalf of the HoD/ Director and its timely submission to e-nba. S/he will be bridging the academic communication between IQAC and concerned faculty members.

d. **Module Coordinator:** S/he is the coordinator of the faculty belonging to a cluster or module of courses. These clusters are properly formulated in the model syllabi developed by AICTE and are available on its website. The abbreviations of such clusters are HS, BS, ES, PC, PE, MC, Project & Training. The coordinator will ensure two communication amongst the module group with the other faculty members in implementing policies and rules within modules and compiling assessment records of students during 8 semesters of the program towards certification of POs.

e. **Course Coordinator:** S/he will coordinate the implementation of modified curriculum by all the faculty members responsible for delivering the common course to students of different branches.

1.3.3. Indicate the additional co-curricular activities undertaken towards the attainment of the PEOs (10)

See also points discussed under 1.3.1

I. **Co-curricular Activities related to the Department or program**

    a. Undertaking assignments for making draft power point presentations for the teacher for classroom and seminar presentations

    b. Searching and compiling trends in some curriculum relevant technologies or process or appliances and helping teacher in preparing review paper for his conference presentation

    c. Contributing to a department project team, by giving manual help in developing/fabricating some experimental apparatus or set-up for doing some R&D / Consultancy projects.

    d. Collecting relevant ideas or problems for major projects during industrial training during 3rd year of BE.

    e. Imparting discipline relevant training or awareness orientation to community mechanics or general public.

II. **Co-curricular activities related to interdisciplinary areas**

    a. Becoming an active member to help in a department project team involved in a problem solving pertaining to interdisciplinary industrial project as a student member.

    b. Developing multidisciplinary application based working Engg models or gadgets for intercollege competition in Automobile Trade fair or Trade exhibitions

    c. Assisting weak learners/ students of junior semesters in some subjects you are very comfortable in time beyond working hours or in the evening hours in the hostel.

d. Participating community services for rendering technical solutions to typical common domestic/ technical problems related to water supply, power supply or in repairing/ explaining desirable approach to repairs of domestic appliances.

III. List of Extra-curricular activities and their functions: These will be chosen as and when necessary for achieving PEOs and POs

- **Sports & Game:** Facing competition, achieving targets, team work & leadership
- **Models making & exhibiting**: Creative designing and fabricating, Problem solving & applying
- **Fine arts exhibits making:** Creativity & personality enrichment
- **Debate, Paper /report writing and seminar presentations:** Confidence, Language proficiency, search & Communication skills
- **Class Monitor:** Leadership and skills to discipline peer team
- **General and industrial visit report writing:** Attitudinal & Language enrichment & behavioral & Communication skills
- **Robotics and avionics:** Analyzing complex scientific phenomena
- **NCC & camping:** Military work culture & ethics, subordination
- **NSS, & performance arts: Drama, dance, painting, cartoons, satires, mimicries**: Sensitivity to Social, ethical and environmental issues & solution

1.4. Assessment of the achievement of the Program Educational Objectives (25)

Define the performance Indicators of PEOs and goals for the attainment of each PEO.

Based on above a comprehensive system of assessment shall be designed and developed which shall be comprising of many processes such as summative and continuous assessment of students' performances and accomplishments, using traditional direct and indirect instruments of assessment as well as newer assessment tools like assessment rubrics and rating scales.

Stake holders like Alumni and employers survey shall generate the most useful data for judging the achievements implied in the PEOs.

The assessment of PEOs can be supplemented by the following data collection and analysis of data:

1. **Indicators of career selection and growth by graduates:**

    a. The PEOs can be judged only when we conduct & collect data from the employer and alumni survey done after 4 +3 or 4 = 7 or 8 years for the batch who has sought admission in the current academic year. Indicators may be that 40% will pursue Sector X or Y.

    b. The Sectors of graduates career selection/ growth can be compared with our today's prediction. Variations shall be bound to be there, but if the variations are too much then we can conclude that our predictions were not very much accurate and are not based on the predictions of market trends about 7 to 8 years back in the past. This includes both wage and self-employed graduates (alumni)

2. **Indicators of growth in Higher education & research by graduates**

    a. The pursuing the options in academics or R&D etc can also be concluded in a similar way.

    b. Some of the accomplishments may be number of technical or research based papers published in the national or international Journals.

    c. How the career as faculty grew by promotions in every 5 years or so?

    d. Number of projects guided of M tech and PhD scholars etc.

    e. Rating of the College he or she is heading.

    f. Number of patents in first ten years of R&D career. & so on…

Therefore, we should look into Central Government's 5 years plans, Upcoming industries, vacancies in new avenues etc., reports of CII, FICII, etc., surveys conducted by mass media agencies etc. before arriving at the contents of PEOs.

1.4.1. Indicate the tools and processes used in assessment of the achievement of the PEOs (15)

The Assessment Process Aspects:

1. The IQAC and Finishing School shall be developing a detailed assessment Policy and Procedure document for this purpose, manage and monitor the implementation of the continuous and terminal assessment system.
2. As and when required proper training of the faculty shall also be undertaken frequently.
3. This system shall include the following regulations

   - Existing Regulations of the University related to Term work marks as well as terminal exam marks mostly related to theory, tutorial and lab/workshop courses. The marks will be sent to the university vide the related regulations and also recorded in the individual portfolios of the students.
   - New Regulations related to the continuous and comprehensive assessment of all performances of the students in the class rooms and beyond the class rooms activities. The marks as and when available shall be stored in the students' portfolios.
   - The College will certify those competencies which are not to be certified by the University on the basis of the records available in the students' portfolios as per format developed by IQAC.
   - The total accomplishment of PEOs (& POs) can be judged on the basis of both the Results of the college and university.

1.4.2. Provide the evidence of the achievement of the PEOs (10)

    a.   Estimate the expected level of goal attainment for each of the program educational objective;

    b.   Comprehend inferences of the results of the evaluation processes and an analysis illustrating the extent to which each of the Program Educational Objectives is being attained; and

    c.   Descriptions of how the results are documented and maintained?

Please see also assessment indicators discussed under clause 1.3.1.

Example:

Performance indicators with goals as accomplished by sample alumni

- Level of technical or professional contribution according to employer
  - o   Goal: 90% or more of graduates meet or exceed expectations of

- Percentage of graduates working in technical or professional careers or enrolled in graduate or professional school
  - o   Goal: 90% or more of graduates meet or exceed expectations.

- Percentage who are working towards another degree since graduation
  - o   Goal: 35% or more of graduates meet or exceed expectations

- Percentage who have published a conference or journal article since graduation
  - o   Goal: 12% or more of graduates meet or exceed expectations

- Percentage who have filed for a patent since graduation
  - o   Goal: 7% or more of graduates meet or exceed expectations o

- Percentage who have had a patent granted since graduation
  - o   Goal: 4% or more of graduates meet or exceed expectations

3. **Goals as Indicators of career selection and growth by graduates:**

   a. The PEOs can be judged when we conduct & collect data from the employer and alumni survey done after 4 +3 or 4 = 7 or 8 years for the batch who has sought admission in the current academic year.

   b. The Sectors of graduates' career selection/ growth can be compared with our today's prediction. Variations are bound to be there, but if the variations are too much then we can conclude that our predictions were not very much accurate and are not based on the predictions of market trends about 7 to 8 years back in the past. This includes both wage and self-employed graduates (alumni)

4. **Indicators of growth in Higher education & research by graduates**

   a. The pursuing the options in academics or R&D can also be concluded in a similar way.

Therefore, we should look into Central Government's Five years plans, upcoming industries, vacancies in new avenues etc., reports of chambers of commerce and industries, surveys conducted by mass media agencies & so on before arriving at the estimates of goals of each PEO.

1.5. Indicate how the PEOs have been redefining in the past (10)

Ideas for future reviews:

1. The predictions may be may be accurate within $\pm$ 10 to 15 %, then we can conclude that our initial procedure for evolving PEOs were logical and we shall follow the same process. Otherwise discuss the matter in the ADB and change the procedure.

2. Every year different reports are published. We shall review our PEOs depending upon the variations in our base line data on wage-employment, promotional aspects of entrepreneurship and establishing one's own business or industry, banking & Govt facilitation policies

etc. Can be helpful in estimating scope of employment or engagement in higher education or research & Development

3. The Department advisory board shall bring ideas from the world of work and shall help directly and indirectly in conducting annual search seminars. The search seminars should be participated by diverse stake holders who shall their experiences in career counseling and administration.

4. The program coordinators should keep itself in inter-active touch with HR people and trends in job markets of the country and other countries. He should circulated the inferences of employment requirements and trend reports published from time to time to all the concerned departments.

5.3. TIPS FOR CREATING A SAR: CRITERIA 2: PROGRAM OUTCOMES (PO) (150)

2.1. Definition and Validation of Course Outcomes and Program Outcomes (25)

2.1.1. List the Course Outcomes (COs) and Program Outcomes (POs) (2)

Provide the list of POs and course outcomes in a tabular format having columns as suggested below;

1. Modules (Course Clusters) - HS, BS, ES, PC, PE, OE, PR and MC
2. Courses: Group Physics I & II as one course etc.
3. Course outcomes (COs)
4. Module outcomes (MOs)

Provide another list of Program outcomes (POs) after approval from Department Advisory Board.

Provide reference here of a separate soft excel file comprising of tabular Correlation matrices between different MOs and POs, the table should have the suggested columns for S. No., Module, Courses, COs or MOs, and POs., and number of rows of different Modules, Cos and MOs. This table will show correlation between 1. Cos and POs as well as 2. MOs and POs within each module. This table will also help in planning for implementation of modified curricula and commensurate planning for assessment, its compilation and keeping records of individual students' achievements.

2.1.2. State how and where the POs are published and disseminated (3)

1. In instructional manuals and curriculum docs
2. Dept. Notice Boards and Students Activity Notice Boards
3. Websites: in Departmental section
4. Institute's and Departments' admission and information Broachers
5. Hostel Wing Notice Boards.
6. On department notice & display Boards,
7. In curriculum implementation documents for all the four years
8. On the website section related to the program details
9. In the laboratory manuals and laboratory charts/ posters
10. On displays located on eye catching points of the department

2.1.3. Indicate the processes employed for defining of the POs (5)

Properties of POs

1. Program Outcomes (POs) describe what students should know and be able to do at the end of the program. POs are to be specific, measurable and achievable. In other words; they should reflect what an ideal graduate: 1. ….should know? 2. …can do? & 3. ….. should care about?
2. POs transform the PEOs into specific student performance and behaviors that demonstrate student learning and skill development
3. POs should be in line with GAs of NBA and POs should ensure **global mobility** of graduate.
4. POs should be **SMART: S**PECIFIC, **M**EASURABLE, **A**PPROPRIATE, **R**EALISTIC, **T**IME- SPECIFIC

Process of defining & reviewing POs:

I. Department's Faculty members should have Comprehensive discussions on the outcome based technical education and relationships between the concepts of Vision, Mission, POs and PEOs with the senior faculty members some of whom should have experience in accreditation process.

II. The global mobility of graduates should be the most logical justification to develop POs in alignment with Graduate Attributes (GAs) as recommended in the NBA manual & Washington accord.

III. Faculty members should study a number of examples after downloading some sample POs.

IV. The third & fourth versions of the POs should be edited by HoD and two faculty members together based on the feedback received during interactions with the stake-holders.

V. The final version was edited after a few days and get approved after the comprehensive discussions in DAB meeting and should be used here.

VI. Review of POs should be done annually after discussions with stake holders in view of the feedback collected over a year particularly considering the issues of mobility of graduates across foreign countries.

2.1.4. Indicate how defined POs aligned to Graduate Attributes prescribed by the NBA (10)

The POs defined for the program are aligned with the Graduate Attributes in a tabular format using the suggested columns and rows

o   Columns: S No., GAs., POs: 1 to n
o   Rows: 1-12, GAs: 1 to 12
o   Entries in cells: degree of alignment: S= strong, M= medium, W= weak

2.1.5. Establish the correlation between the POs and the PEOs (5)

Prepare a tabular correlation matrix between POs and PEOs having columns: S No., PEOs, POs= 1 to n and rows: 1 to m, PEOs: 1 to m. Enter into cells degree of correlation- S for strong, M-for medium and W for weak.

2.2. Attainment of Program Outcomes (40)

2.2.1. Illustrate how course outcomes contribute to the POs (10)

Provide the correlation between the course outcomes and the program outcomes. The strength of the correlation may also be indicated. On similar lines as explained in 2.1.5.

There shall be 9 to 12 POs and it is obvious all these POs cannot be developed during learning & teaching processes of one or two courses or within one or two semesters. An innovative instructional planning needs to be made so that a group of 2 or 3 POs can be taken care of during teaching of one course. Acquisition of Such small groups of POs should be frequently repeated during teaching of different courses and thus the selected POs shall get on consolidated due to repeated learning at ever growing levels of complexities of problem solving.

Such innovative instructional strategies should be developed under continuous improvement endeavors along with increasing maturity of students, faculty and institution as a whole.

2.2.2. Explain how modes of delivery of courses help in the attainment of the POs (10)

There shall be 9 to 12 POs and it is obvious all these POs cannot be developed during learning & teaching processes of one or two courses or within one or two semesters. An innovative instructional planning needs to be made so that a group of 2 or 3 POs can be taken care of during teaching of one course. Acquisition of Such small groups of POs should be frequently repeated during teaching of different courses and thus the selected POs shall get on consolidated due to repeated learning at ever growing levels of complexities of problem solving.

Such innovative instructional strategies comprising of combinations of a variety of methods, media, learning resources and communication & information technologies should be developed under continuous improvement endeavors. Its sophistication and novelty of such strategic planning should keep on improving with increasing maturity of students, faculty and institution as a whole.

A combination of direct and indirect assessment tools and instruments including assessment rubrics should be used to assess the performances of both students and faculty in order to effectively assess and provide feedback for appropriate midterm corrections in both teaching and learning techniques and approaches.

General considerations

A1. See clauses 1.3 and 1.4 sections related to attainment of PEOs.

A2. All traditional tests for assessing theoretical knowledge and tests and viva etc. for lab work and project work can be slightly modified and synchronized with assessment of POs

A3. When the instructions of content & their assessment shall be integrated with POs & PEOs, then Assessment Rubrics should be developed, implemented and continuously improved upon over a period of a few semesters.

General Principles (Education Technology) for maximizing the contributions of COs to attain POs

1. All the faculty and Managers of the college be oriented to realize that the BE 1st Year **Students should be treated as adults right from second semester onwards**. The psychology of learning by adults is entirely different as compared to that of children (Pedagogy)

2. **Teach theory courses with a focus on learning by students**. Avoid over teaching and continuous teaching/ lecturing; have breathing spaces for the students activities such as

   a. Encourage self-study based library assignments to develop life-learning habits and desist students to come out of over dependence on internal or external coaches & tutors & their vicious circles which have completely destroyed the self-learning culture amongst students.

   b. Asking questions and seek clarifications on their individual doubts at the end of each period for about 10% of time available.

c. Give some oral or written quizzes or tests and allow them to answer.

d. Ask some of them to come to the board and write something to facilitate their explanation.

e. Ask them to participate in classroom demonstrations and seminars and compete for best presentation awards.

f. Have tutorial classes regularly and give students library reading assignments before attending the tutorial classes.

g. Regularly have the unit tests and discuss the kinds of common mistakes committed by students in tutorial class and let them solve the full paper again.

h. Keep full Saturday as a self-learning in library day and award sessional marks for their attendance & minimum days count in the library.

i. Keep the library operational at least 3 hours beyond the working hours and regulate the part of bus transportation to facilitate transportation of students in late hours after library self-studies.

3. undertaken by the students beyond theory classes and develop a transparent comprehensive as well as continuous assessment criteria sets for assessment of different types of activities having potential towards building up their professional personalities. Keep record of results of such assessment in the individual portfolio of every student and give marks and grades to them on the bases of info available in the portfolio.

4. Identify and list all the possible and potential activities All such modes of delivery should be assessed by requesting students to express their opinions about their satisfaction level during exit of a semester.

The department & faculty should keep secured records of continuous & terminal assessment of students' performances in their personal portfolios for both theory and experiential learning

The assessment Rubrics shall be optimized when the institute shall develop suitable IT tools to make entries and collate results on the basis of incidental observations of behavior of students and using their individual portfolios

for record keeping and compilation of final assessment & joint certification by the University & the College.

Please refer to the diagram 2.2. The Figure illustrates interrelationship between different concepts defining outcome based professional higher education system.

2.2.3. Indicate the extent to which the laboratory and project course work are contributing towards the attainment of the POs (20)

Analyze your current syllabi as well as model syllabi developed by AICTE and determine the ratio of credits allocated to Lab & Project work inputs to credits allocated to Theoretical inputs. Keep record of this tabular analysis for future reference.

You might conclude that about 30% credits are allocated to the practical work inputs in the curricular activities.

Practical work inputs are important for developing back ground knowledge, performing techniques, skills and attitudes. It is helpful to practice a skill in different situations again and again to improve the competence and confidence of performing like a professional.

POs are the statements of graduates' entry level competencies of a professional Engineer and therefore the importance of Laboratory and Project work becomes quite important in acquiring problem diagnostic and solving skills.

If you find that your existing curriculum does not have a provision of 30% of total credits for practical work then introduce extra experiments and assignments to compensate the deficiency. For NBA accreditation & Washington accord attainment of all the POs should be treated as mandatory for ensuring global mobility.

Laboratory work-experience develops the abilities of using technical techniques in performing general technical tasks, working in teams & leadership qualities, housekeeping, etc. applying basic and Engg Sc and techniques in solving relatively well defined problems, writing reports, presenting orally & in writing technical reports, concepts and laws, interpretation of results and reinforcement of theory learned in the classrooms.

Workshop Skills: Demonstrates the application of theoretical concepts in machines and equipment. **It** makes aware of safety and dimensional quality assurance concepts along with practice in using relevant hand-tools and simpler machine tools and a set of techniques to perform a technical task.

Project Work: it consolidates the application of Science & Engg & technology in comprehending a problem and its dimensions and parameters. It develops ability to understand & write specifications, resources and constraints of a relatively open ended technical problem. It trains in creative yet systematic design of Engg Solutions considering diverse and conflicting criteria and considerations.

It trains in problem solving competence and communication skills (thinking & writing, making presentation materials, presenting the experiences of problem solving, defending the approach of the problem solving & so on... It develops confidence and entry professional personality preparing the person to face the real-life problems, leadership, team work and confidence to handle complex situations etc.

2.3. Evaluation of the attainment of Program Outcomes (75)

2.3.1. Describe assessment tools and processes used for assessing the attainment of each PO (50)

Describe the assessment process that periodically documents and demonstrate the degree to which the Program Outcomes are attained.
Also include information on:

- A listing and description of the assessment processes should use to collect the data & information upon which the graduates' evaluation of achievements related to each of the Program Outcome is based. Examples of data collection processes may include, but are not limited to, specific examination questions, student portfolios, internally developed assessment examinations, major project presentations, nationally-normed exams, oral exams, focus groups, reports of industrial advisory committee etc.
- The listing should also include the frequency with which these assessment processes are carried out within a semester.
- List of ASSESSMENT TOOLS & Particulars {Components of Assessment Rubrics} may include some of the following;

AST 1.   Objective Questions test or Short Answer Questions test

AST 2.   End of term Test

AST 3.   Performing a Lab Experiment

AST 4.   Check list for Interview or Oral Viva Voce with visuals

AST 5.   Check list for Observing of a group Discussion

AST 6.   Assessing on: Self-study efforts in library, making a PPP, & presentation of seminar on allotted topic to classroom.

AST 7.   Data from alumni survey or Employer Survey

AST 8.   Rating scale for assessing design based problem solving.

AST 9.   A: Rating Scale for assessing performance of a Design task, team work and leadership qualities or B: Rating scale for assessing Project Management skills: Analyzing the given problem, dividing it into parts, distributing the parts to the team members to work on parts, hold meetings and consultations, attending to individual difficulties, assembling the solution, testing the solution, identifying minor issues, distributing the issues to team members, preparing the problem – solution report and PPP, making presentations, receiving feedback and submitting the final report at the completion of the project.

You should present another tabular matrix correlating the assessment instruments /tools with related POs by displaying tests along rows and POs along one column after discussing the matrix with all related faculty members and allied managers.

2.3.2. Indicate results of evaluation of each PO (25)

The results of assessment of each PO should try to mention most of the following aspects.

a.   The expected level of attainment for each of the Program Outcomes;

b.   Summaries of the results of the evaluation processes and an analysis illustrating the extent to which each of the program outcomes are attained; and

c. How the results are documented and maintained.

Accomplishment of all POs or competencies have four dimensions:

Knowledge outcomes: what a graduate knows?- understanding fundamental concepts & relationships, basic inquiry and search skills to get more related info.

Mental Skills outcomes: Applying basic principles of Basic Science, Engineering Science, Professional core & elective course in comprehending and solving an open ended problem, defining it with its boundary conditions, identifying possible solutions, selecting a pragmatic solution and trying to further apply selected solution, present and defend the solution & so on..

Attitudes & Values Outcomes: Personal, Professional and ethical values & preferences.

Behavioral Outcomes: the ways of a person behaves with peers, superiors and inferiors in normal life is the manifestation of the learned outcomes of knowledge, skills and values. These are valuable indicators of levels of professional personality development.

Therefore a variety of direct and indirect methods of assessment shall be used to assess the different dimensions of each POs. We shall design an assessment Rubric for each PO where contributions of tests results / indicators for **knowledge, skills, values & behavior** shall be collated together to arrive at the final measure or grade of PO.

2.4. Indicate how the results of evaluation of achievement of the Pos have been used for redefining the POs (10)

A review system shall be developed on the bases of experiencing of confronting the operational and reporting issues after implementation for some period.

A system of reviewing shall be developed by ACDAC & FS (see section 1.3.2) in near future after gaining some experience in the area of continuous assessment using direct and indirect methods as elaborated above.

5.4: TIPS FOR CRITERIA-3

3.0: Program Curriculum (125)

3.1. Curriculum (15)

a. Describe the structure of the curriculum (5)

Mention the time duration in Hours and value of credits allocated to different course clusters for Learning-teaching sessions (L), Tutorials/ seminars (T), Practical/ lab/ projects (P), ratio between L & (T+P) in the format provided.

You should refer to section 4.3 for more information about modifying curriculum in chapter 4 to answer queries of this section.

3.1.2. Give the Prerequisite flow chart of courses (5)

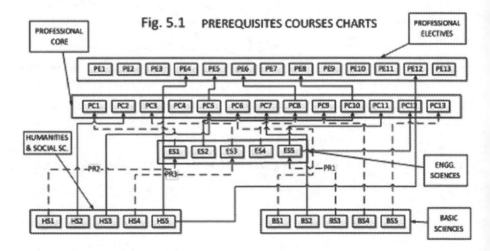

Fig. 5.1   PREREQUISITES COURSES CHARTS

This is a graphic designed on MS Visio software. You can fill the course codes of your syllabi in place of the cluster specific names shown here such as ES3 & PC 4 etc. The prerequisite course forms the platform for understanding and learning an Engg. Science course or an advanced technology course.

3.1.3. Justify how the program curriculum satisfies the program specific criteria (5)

(Justify how the program curriculum satisfies the program specific criteria specified by the American professional societies relevant to the program under accreditation)

1. Search of Program Specific Criteria: Go to website: www.abet.org and down load document: **"Criteria for accrediting engineering programs or ABET Criteria- 2013-2014"**
2. Search the compatible program with your program and
3. Then prepare a table of correlation between your program PEOs with the Criteria of ABET's Criteria.

3.1.4: Correlation table between PEOs & specific criteria

Prepare a tabular matrix having column components: PEO No., PEO Statement, Part of specific Criteria, value of Correlation.

3.2. State the components of the curriculum and their relevance to the POs and the PEOs (15)

Prepare a table as per format suggested in the SAR format.

3.3. State core engineering subjects and their relevance to Program outcomes including design experience (30)

Prepare a table having columns: Course code of professional courses, title of course, POs = 1 to n and rows Professional courses, Cell entry: value of relevance as S/M/W.

Where; Strong Relevance=S, Moderate Relevance=M, Weak Relevance=W for developing abilities of solving open ended complex engineering problems.

3.4. Industry interaction/internship (10)

(Give the details of industry involvement in the program such as industry-attached laboratories and partial delivery of courses and internship opportunities for students)

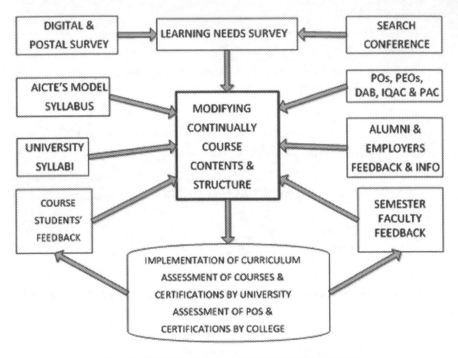

Fig. 5.2: CURRICULUM DEVELOPMENT MODEL

ASPECTS OF INDUSTRY INSTITUTE PARTNERSHIP: Table Rows= Orientation lectures, delivering Content Lectures, Curriculum Development, Training of Faculty, Training of technical Staff, Training/internship of Students, Contributions in major Project work, Participation in R&D, Placements & sharing info on employment trends' projections, Regular Employers feedback surveys, Participation in Seminars.

3.5.1. State the process of designing program curriculum (5)

The above mentioned diagram illustrates the aspects to be considered while formulating the modifications in the existing syllabi of the affiliating university. You may describe your syllabi modification process based on this basic model with your own creativity, experience and circumstances.

3.5.2. State the measures and processes used to improve courses and curriculum. (10)

Course Content and improving its delivery:

1. Focus on learning by students. For achieving this, try to understand & practice the psychology of learning by adults or Andragogy. The following are the important principles to be internalized by heart by all the faculty members of higher education. Please you are dealing with adults and adults learn in entirely different ways as compared to children.

1.1: **Instructional design Principles based on ANDRAGOGY (Psychology of Learning by Adults)**

- *Adults need to be involved in the planning and evaluation of their instruction.*
- *Experience (including mistakes) provides the basis for learning activities.*
- *Adults are most interested in learning mental & manual skills that have immediate relevance to their job or personal life. This is the biggest reason for their intrinsic motivation to learn.*
- *Adult learning is problem-centered rather than content-oriented. If you force teaching and teaching schedule as desired by you or management then the effectiveness and*

2. **Motivation:** Establish the relevance & importance of your course in their possible job situations to keep them motivated and interested to learn what you wish them to learn. Keep on repeating this relevance from time to time.

3. **Planning:** Try to plan out interactive academic activities with students such as group discussions/ games, competitive classroom Seminars, discussions on typical questions & solutions relevant to

course assessment, active tutorials, conflicting design considerations, technology and its impact on environment and economy etc.

4. **Giving due importance to Problem based learning-teaching:**

    a. Adults learn better when they struggle for learning. Problem solving opportunities to students with restricted guidance makes them a better professional and much ready to work in industry.

    b. Major project is an open ended problem solving. Encourage students to select some realistic or industrial problem and monitor their learning progress from a safe distance.

5. **Extracurricular activities:** Encourage students to undertake extra-curricular activities to enrich their professional personalities.

6. **Integrated Assessment:** Connect & correlate relevant POs & PEOs with lab, industrial visits/ training and Project work and perform students' continuous direct / indirect assessment with integrated criteria for technical competence as well as professional competence in their performance & behavior.

7. **Finishing School & Engg Department:**

    a. Share responsibilities with FS in facilitating students in attainment of POs & PEOs. And employability skills.

    b. Keep **active communications** with FS to keep updated with the trends in employment requirements and keep on correlating curricular reforms & entrepreneurship development with employment.

    c. Cooperate with FS in facilitating the processes of on/off campus placement of your graduates as well as in selecting industry relevant major project work

8. **Action Research: exploit the following opportunities & publish research papers in Education Technology Journals;**

    a. Effect of changes in methods and media of course delivery on learning by students.

   b.   Continuously keep on improving the assessment formats and approaches to make it more and more precise and objective.

   c.   Keep on Improving the survey instruments and their data analysis methods

   d.   Improving the faculty competence and commitments towards students & royalty towards management.

9.   **Encourage self-learning groups** both in the faculty and students for continuous development by their peer group.

   a.   Students shall become a better **life-long learners**

   b.   Faculty shall become a better **life-long learner cum effective teacher.**

3.6. Course Syllabi (5)

The syllabi format may include:

- Department, course number, and title of course
- Designation as a required or elective course
- Pre-requisites
- Contact hours and type of course (lecture, tutorial, seminar, project etc.)
- Course Outcomes
- Hints for course assessment methods (both continuous and semester-end assessment)
- Hints for Course delivery methods
- Topics covered
- Text books, and/or reference material

Modified Format of NBA Syllabus- (commensurate with latest info by NBA)

- Department, Course Number and title of Course
- Identification of Course Designers: names of faculty (writers & editors) with designations & qualifications

o Mapping with Faculty Expertise (total experience and experience of teaching compatible course)

- Designation as a Core or Elective course
- Pre-requisites
- Contact Hours and type of course (Lecture, tutorial, seminar, project, etc)
- Course Assessment Methods (Both Continuous and Semester-end Assessment)
- Course Outcomes
- Topics Covered
- Extra topics and practical work experience added
- Text Books and/or Reference Material for further self-study.

5.5: LIST OF RECORDS FILES & EXHIBITS FOR SHOWING EVIDENCES DURING INSPECTION

The following is the list of files in which record of past three years of performance are compiled. Some of the files present expansion of the sample tabular information and factual information which is required by & presented in the SAR. Only a brief sample of such information is illustrated in SAR to keep it short and to the point. Such information should be compiled such that the information related to all the 8 semesters are covered.

A. List of Institutional Record Files:

IN.1. Land papers, built-plan and approval etc.

IN.2. Composition of Governing Council/ Board/Body, Senate and other Academic and Administrative bodies, their functions and responsibilities. List of all the meetings held in the past 3 years along with the attendance records. Representative minutes and action-taken reports of a few meetings of such bodies along with the list of current faculty members who are members of such bodies.

IN.3. Rules, policies and procedures published by the Institution including service book and academic regulations and other along with the proof that the employees/students are aware of the rules and procedures.

IN.4. Budgeted allocation and utilization: Audited statement of accounts

IN.5. Informative web site

IN.6. Library resources – books and journal holdings,

IN.7. Listing of core, computing and manufacturing etc. labs (list of Clusters with included courses)

IN.8. Records of T & P and career and guidance cells

IN.9. Records of safety checks and critical installations (Preparedness for Disaster Management)

IN.10. Medical care records and usages of ambulance etc.

IN.11. Academic calendar, schedule of tutorial and makeup classes

IN.12. Handouts/ files along with Outcomes; list of additional topics to meet the outcomes. (Referring to courses)

IN.13. Set of question papers, assignments, evaluation schemes etc. (IN.11+IN.12+IN.13 = Course Files)

IN.14. Feedback form, analysis of feedback and corrective actions

IN.15. Documented feedback received from the stake-holders (e.g., Industries, Parents, Alumni, and Financiers etc.) of the Institution

IN.16. List of faculty who teach first year courses along with their qualifications

IN.17. Results of the First Year students.

B. List of Program Specific Record Files;

Each program for which an institution seeks accreditation or re-accreditation should prepare the following record files:

PS.1 NBA accreditation reports of the past visits, if any

PS.2 Department budget and allocations of the (past 3 years data)

PS.3 Admission – seats filled and ranks (last 3 years data)

PS.4 List/ Number of students who clear the program in 4years (last 3 years data)

P.5 CGPA -Average Grade point (last 3 years data of students' CGPA/ percentage)

PS.6 Placement and higher studies data (last 3 years data)

PS.7   Professional society activities, events, conferences organized etc. (Including Students' Chapters)

PS.8   List of students' papers along with hard-copies of the publications; professional society publications/ magazines, etc.

PS.9   Sample best and average project reports/theses

PS.10 Details of faculty student ratio

PS.11 Faculty details with their service books, salary details, sample appointment letters, promotion and award letters/certificates

PS.12 Faculty list with designation, qualification, joining date, publication, R & D, interaction details

PS.13 List of faculty publications along with DOIs and publication/ citation details

PS.14 List of R & D and consultancy projects along with approvals and project completion reports

PS.15 List and proofs of faculty interaction with outside world

PS.16 List of class rooms, faculty rooms,

PS.17 List of program specific labs and computing facility within department.

PS.18 List of non-teaching staff with their appointment letters etc

PS.19 List of short-term courses, workshop arranged and course-modules developed

PS.20 Records of new program specific facility created, if any

PS.21 Records of overall program specific improvements, if any

PS.22 Curriculum, PEOs and Outcomes, (All curricula semester wise booklets in format suggested in SAR)

PS.23 Correlation / Mapping of Program Outcomes with PEOs (Excel Sheets)

PS.24 Correlation / Mapping of courses/ course with Program Outcomes (Excel Sheets)

PS.25 Course files, plan of course delivery, question papers, answer scripts, assignments, reports of assignments, project reports, reports of design projects, list of lab experiments, reports of lab experiments, etc.

PS.26 Rubrics developed to validate the POs.

PS.27 Continuous improvements in PEOs

PS.28 Improvements in curriculum for correlation / mapping POs and PEOs

PS.29 Direct and indirect assessment methods to show attainment of POs

PS.30 Stake-holders involvement in the process of improvement of PEOs and POs

PS.31 Collected Forms of indirect assessment tools (e.g- alumni survey, employer survey)

PS.32 Any other document which may be necessary to evaluate the SAR.

C. List of Program Specific Exhibits (Files):

EP1.   Profile of faculty involved in the program

EP2.   Evidence that the results of assessment of course outcomes and program outcomes are being applied to the review and ongoing improvement of program effectiveness

EP3.   list of publications, consultancy and sponsored/funded research projects by programme faculty

EP4.   Sample materials for theory and laboratory courses

EP5.   Sample test /semester examination question papers for all courses

EP6.   Sample of test/semester examination answer scripts projects, assignments, (including at least one excellent, one good and one marginal pass for each examination) question papers and evidences related to assessment tools for COs and POs

EP7.   Student records of three immediate batches of graduates

EP8.   Sample project and design reports (excellent, good and marginal pass) by students

EP9.   Sample student feedback form

EP10. Sample for industry- institute interaction

EP11. Results of quality assurance reviews

EP12. Records of employment/higher studies of graduates

EP13. Records of academic support and other learning activities

EP14. Any other documents that the Evaluation Team/NBA may request

Although, the preparation of SAR should be given top priority, but initiating preparation of above record files is very important so that whatever can be accessed during completion of SAR can be collected in these files which can be organized later on as per chronological order. However, completion of these files in all r respect must be taken up with full attention just after the on-line uploading of the e-SAR in the institutional folder on the website of e-NBA.

There shall be doubts about the formats of presenting data, which can be sorted as per directions given by DAB and IQAC.

5.6: IMPORTANT QUESTIONS ROR MANAGERS, FACULTY AND STUDENTS;

The following are the exhaustive list of important questions which can be asked by the NBA Inspection team from different stakeholders. These questions are illustrative, not exhaustive. The visiting team members are encouraged to frame their own questions with the basic objective of interviewing the stakeholders.

Questions to the Head of Institution

1. How is an equitable distribution of funds to departments ensured?
2. How does research activity have linkages and benefits to the undergraduate program?
3. Do research scholars and PG students conduct tutorials and laboratory demonstration?
4. Do they receive any training?
5. What are the faculties' workloads like?
6. How do you balance teaching and research?
7. What are the strategic directions for engineering?
8. Tell us the direction in which engineering is headed at your institution.
9. Is the current level of industry inputs towards program design and targeted graduate outcomes adequate?

Questions to the Dean / Head of Department / Program Coordinators

1. How is the academic faculty involved in program design?
2. How can the level of faculty development be adapted to improve quality of teaching?

3. How many members of the faculty are involved in such activity?
4. How many members of the faculty are involved in an internship scheme?
5. What is the procedure for securing leave for the purpose of study?
6. How many members of the faculty are involved in the Foundations of Teaching and Learning program?
7. Describe your role and responsibilities.
8. How many members of the faculty are involved in the academic leadership course for Course Coordinators?
9. How is the program review initiated and implemented? When does industry interaction begin?
10. What is the degree and extent of the faculties' involvement in program review?
11. Tell us about the balance between the coverage of discipline-specific and engineering practice in the First Year.
12. What are the strategic directions for engineering?
13. How do you feel about the quality of laboratories and the level of student engagement?
14. To what extent are laboratories and facilities useful for practical learning and project work?
15. What might be the development directions and prioritization?
16. Is the quantum and quality of laboratory practice consistent with the needs of an engineering graduate?
17. Are the laboratory equipment and computers maintained properly?
18. Is the supporting staff adequate for these activities?
19. Are you aware of the specified program outcomes?
20. What progress has been made on tracking the development, throughout the program, of graduate attributes?
21. What do you see as the positives associated with this program?
22. What are the characteristics that make this program good or unique?
23. What are your views of the capabilities of your students at the time of completion of their studies?
24. What are your views on the employability of your students?
25. Where is professional development being delivered (writing, communication and research skills, teamwork, project management, etc)? Is it embedded throughout the program?

26. Is there sufficient elective choice for the student in the program? Could it be enhanced? Is the development of engineering design skills adequate?
27. How is design embedded into the program?
28. How are the issues of engineering ethics, sustainability and environment covered throughout the program?
29. Are the students exposed to issues related to globalization and changing technologies?
30. What proportion of final year projects is industry-based?
31. How are they supervised and managed?
32. What proportion of final year projects is research-oriented?
33. Is the course material made available to students?
34. Where do students perform their assignment work?
35. Is the working space for group work available separately?
36. What are the modern tools used for teaching?
37. Are students able to learn better from power point presentations?
38. How much exposure do you allow for local industry practices, such as guest presentations, teaching by visiting faculty, site visits, industry problem solving, case studies, and industry projects occurring?
39. Are these events prescribed as part of the overall educational design, or simply included on the initiative of the local program/course coordinator?
40. How is the exposure to professional practice monitored and assessed?
41. What kinds of site visits are offered? Are these site visits arranged for the students?
42. What kinds of opportunities are being grasped in industrial design and project work to take advantage of industry topics or input?
43. Are industry-based projects supervised or co-supervised by industry people?
44. Does industry sponsor the project work?
45. Do all students undertake an internship or industrial training?
46. Describe the reporting mechanisms and assessment requirements.
47. What are the overall quality mechanisms that ensure appropriateness of outcomes?
48. How is the academic faculty involved in achievement of the Graduate Attributes?

49. What efforts are made to ensure that assessment truly assesses the student learning outcomes in each subject?
50. How are the Course Outcomes and assessment measures at the unit level tracked to close the loop on delivery of targeted graduate outcomes?
51. What are the roles of the Program Coordinator, course coordinators and academic faculty in program review and quality improvement?
52. How often does the faculty meet as a teaching team to discuss program improvement issues?
53. To what extent are improvements made from student feedback?
54. Are unit outlines demonstrating closure of the quality loop at unit and program levels?
55. State the level of industry input to program design and targeted graduate outcomes.
56. What is the impact of the advisory committee on contextualizing the program to local and global needs?
57. What are the mechanisms available for formal/documented student feedback? How is student feedback obtained?
58. Do students receive feedback on actions taken?
59. Are issues of graduate outcomes, curriculum design and improvement discussed?
60. What other consultation mechanisms are available?
61. How does the faculty respond to the outcomes of student/unit surveys?
62. What changes have been made to the program as a result of your evaluation?
63. What is the process used for making changes to the program outcomes?
64. How do the faculty credentials relate to the PEOs and the POs?
65. Is the quantum and quality of laboratory practice consistent with the needs of an engineering graduate?
66. How active is the industry-institute interaction partnership cell?
67. What kind of changes has been made in the program from the inputs of the industry-institute interaction partnership cell?
68. What are the strengths and weaknesses of your department, and the supporting departments?
69. Have any major curriculum changes been planned? What are they? When do they come into effect?

70. What are the major needs for growth and development of the curriculum?
71. Do you make recommendations for faculty salary and increments? How much time does a faculty member have for professional development?
72. What is the budget for faculty professional development?
73. Are faculty sent abroad under faculty exchange program?

Questions to faculty

1. How does research activity have linkages and benefits to undergraduate program?
2. Do research scholars and PG students conduct tutorials and laboratory demonstration?
3. Do they receive any training?
4. How do you ensure that appropriate assessment techniques are being used?
5. What assessment moderation processes are used? Is there any senior project work?
6. What professional development (T&L-related) have you received?
7. What are faculty workloads like? How do you balance your teaching and research?
8. What are the good things that are happening in the program?
9. What are the unwanted things that are happening in the program?
10. What program educational objectives and program outcomes do the courses you teach support?
11. Are you involved in the assessment/evaluation of program educational objectives and program outcomes? How?
12. Are you involved in program improvements? In what capacity?
13. Is there sufficient elective choice for the student in the program? Could it be made better?
14. How is the Honors program different from the graduate program?
15. Is the development of engineering design skills adequate? How is design embedded into the program?
16. How are the issues of engineering ethics, sustainability and environment, and business studies covered throughout the program?

17. Are the students exposed to issues related to globalization and changing technologies?
18. What proportions of final year projects are industry-based? How are they supervised and managed?
19. Are lectures recorded and made available to students?
20. How do you ensure that appropriate assessment techniques are being used?
21. How much time do you spend on professional development?
22. What professional society are you a member of? Are you active? Do you hold any office?
23. Does the same instructor teach both lecture and laboratory portions of related courses? If not, how do they coordinate?
24. Is the salary structure satisfactory?
25. What additional benefits have been included?
26. What unique or unusual teaching methods are being used in your department?
27. Do you maintain regular contacts with industry? How?
28. How has the industrial-institute partnership cell affected the POs?
29. Are the support departments providing appropriate educational services for your students?
30. Is there adequate secretarial and technical service available to you?
31. Have you acquired any additional qualification to provide effective teaching?
32. How is your industrial experience, if any, relevant to this program?
33. What is your role in the continuous improvement of the program?
34. What are the roles of the Head of the Department, Course coordinators and staff members in program review and quality improvement?
35. How often does the staff meet as a teaching team to discuss program improvement issues?
36. What are the other consultation/grievances mechanisms available?

Questions to students

1. Has your educational experience measured up to your expectations?
2. Comment on facilities such as laboratory, IT access, information resources and project work.

3. Have you provided feedback as part of a quality/programme improvement mechanism?

4. To what extent does the programme provide for your personal and professional capability development?

5. Have measures been taken for your personal development and performance such as team-work, leadership, management, communication and presentation skills, self-learning capacity etc?

6. Are these systematically addressed in the subjects?

7. Have issues such as globalization, ethics and sustainable practices been addressed yet?

8. What improvement would you make if you had a magic wand?

9. Did you make use of online learning facilities? What are they? Do they make a difference?

10. Do you feel that you have an understanding of the targeted outcomes for your programme and the real nature of engineering practice in your chosen domain?

11. How was this understanding established?

12. How successful are faculty members as role models of the professional engineer?

13. How accessible is the faculty?

14. Did you get exposure to sessions or guest lectures by practicing professionals? Are these well-organized and well-presented?

15. According to you, what are the key attributes an employer would be looking for in a graduate engineer?

16. How effective are subject/unit outline documents in communicating and interlinking objectives, learning outcomes, activities and assessment strategies within individual units? Within academic units,

17. Is assessment well-coordinated with objectives and targeted learning outcomes?

18. Are there other avenues of embedded professional practice exposure other than placement activities, such as industry visits, field trips, industry assignments, case studies, industry based projects etc.?

19. Is there sufficient exposure to professional practice?

20. How effective is laboratory learning?

21. Are experiments prescriptive or open-ended?

22. What has been the nature of project-based learning activity in the program?

23. Have you been confronted with multi-disciplinary, open-ended, complex projects?

24. Has it been necessary to consider factors such as social, environmental, safe practices and ethical matters?

25. Have you been involved in any team-based learning activities yet? Have you become a good team player and/or team leader?

26. Have you been assessed for your team performance?

27. What input do you have for the quality system, the processes of educational design and continuous improvement?

28. Is your feedback effective?

29. Does it bring about change?

30. Do you hear about improvement being made?

31. What skills are you expected to acquire at the time of graduation? Comment on the attainment of the program educational objectives.

32. To what extent does the program provide for your personal and professional capabilities development?

33. Are there measures of your personal development and performance such as team-work, leadership, management, communication and presentation skills, self-learning capacity etc.?

34. Are these systematically addressed in subjects?

35. Are you acquiring the expected / required skills?

36. Are the faculty members competent in the subjects they teach?

37. Are faculty members helpful and available at times convenient for you?

38. Why did you choose this institution/department / program?

39. Are the laboratory equipment/tools/accessories well-maintained?

40. How would you rate the hands-on experience?

41. Do you plan to continue your education after graduation? Where? When?

42. Do you plan to accept a job after graduation? Where? When?

43. What type of job can you get as a graduate of this program?

44. What salary do you expect?

45. What is your overall view of the program?

46. Would you recommend it to a friend?

47. Are you providing feedback as part of a quality/program improvement mechanism?

Please note that the collection of data for completing the above mentioned Institution specific, Program specific and exhibit related record files is a huge and complex task which must be executed by the HoD and some other senior faculty members. Program coordinator should completely be relieved from this task.

The director and HoDs should also prepare points and hints for answering above mentioned large number of questions by different groups of stakeholders. Every group should be oriented about possible answers for relevant questions. If you leave this task to the common sense of stake holder groups then their self-contradicting answers may spoil all efforts done in preparing SAR as well as efforts made by the managers and program coordinators for impressing the NBA's inspection team.

This task is indeed is quite complex, but is important and shall require all your creativity and intelligence to complete to your own satisfaction. Remember these record files shall be equally useful for acquiring accreditation from NAAC and any other international accreditation agency.

CHAPTER 6.0

ACCREDITATION OF DIPLOMA IN ENGINEERING & TECHNOLOGY PROGRAMS

6.1: Accreditation criteria for Diploma in Engg & Technology
6.2: Level of learning outcomes for Diploma in Engg & Technology
6.3: Tips to respond to typical portions of the SAR except accreditation criteria.
6.4: Tips for preparing typical record files related to institute and program

6.1: ACCREDITATION CRITERIA FOR DIPLOMA IN ENGG & TECHNOLOGY

A diploma engineering program to be accredited or reaccredited shall have to satisfy all the criteria during the full term of accreditation. The educational institution should periodically review the strength and weakness of the program, seek to improve standards and quality continually and to address deficiencies if any aspect falls short of the standards set by the accreditation criteria. During the full term of accreditation, the institutions are required to submit their annual self-assessment report to NBA on-line.

The criteria of Tier-I & Tier-II for Diploma in Engg. & Technology are the same as were for Bachelor of Engg & technology programs. The question arises then how one can differentiate between the graduates of Bachelor and Diploma level programs. This understanding shall be helpful in preparing the PEOs and POs at Diploma level accreditation. The criteria are slightly different for tier-I (autonomous) and Tier-II (non-autonomous) Diploma programs.

#	Criteria Class of Institution	Marks Maximum & Minimum T-I	T-II
1.	Vision, Mission & PEOs	75 & 45	75 & 45
2.	**Program outcomes**	**225 & 135**	**200 & 120**
3.	Program Curriculum	100 & 60	100 & 60
4.	Students' Performance	100 & 60	100 & 60
5.	Faculty Contributions	100 & 60	100 & 60
6.	Facilities and Technical Support	100 & 60	100 & 60
7.	Academic Support Units and Teaching-Learning processes	150 & 90	150 & 90
8.	**Governance, Institutional Support and Financial Resources**	**75 & 45**	**100 & 60**
9.	Continuous Improvement	75 & 45	75 & 45
•	Total score (For Tier-I)	1000 & 600	

• Total score (for Tier- II):
  o if score is more than 750 with minimum of 60% in mandatory criteria 1 & 4 to 8, accreditation is awarded for 5 years
  o If score is between 600 & 750 with 60% score in mandatory criteria 1 & 4 to 8, accreditation is awarded for 2 years.

The criteria of program outcomes have been given slightly more weight (225-200) for autonomous institutions whereas criteria of governance, institutional support & financial resources have been given more weight (100-75) in case of non-autonomous institutions. In other words, the autonomous institutions should care more for program outcomes which should be possible for them due to better faculty & financial resources and more academic autonomy, where as non-autonomous institutions should improve their governance and management of human and financial resources.

6.2: LEVELS OF LEARNING OUTCOMES FOR DIPLOMA IN ENGINEERING & TECHNOLOGY PROGRAMS

A document with the title of '**Graduate Attributes and Professional Competencies**' has been developed & published by International Engineering Alliance (www.washingtonaccord.org) which describes the competency profiles of engineering & technology pass-outs accomplishing graduations from there different levels of qualifications namely 1. Bachelor Degree in Engg. & tech. or {(E&T), (10+2+4) years}, 2. Diploma in Engg. & tech. (10+3 years) and 3. Certificate in Engg. & Tech. trades (10/12+2 years). The best way to understand the difference between the competencies of graduates of a Bachelor and Diploma level programs is to the following competency profiles related to *Graduate Attributes (GAs)* developed for these two different qualified graduates. Italic fonts have been used to highlight the points of difference.

Serial Number notations: *WA* prefix has been used to number GAs of Bachelor of E&T: (Washington Accord-WA) and *SA* to represent GAs of diploma of E&T (Sydney Accord-SA)

WA1: Apply knowledge of mathematics, natural science, engineering fundamentals and an engineering specialization *to the solution of complex engineering problems.*

SA1: Apply knowledge of mathematics, natural science, engineering fundamentals and an engineering specialization **to defined and applied engineering procedures, processes, systems or methodologies.**

WA2: Identify, formulate, research literature and analyze *complex engineering problems* reaching substantiated conclusions using first principles of mathematics, natural sciences and engineering sciences.

SA2: Identify, formulate, research literature and analyze **broadly-defined engineering problems** reaching substantiated conclusions using analytical tools appropriate to the discipline or area of specialization.

WA3: Design solutions for *complex engineering problems and design systems,* components or processes that meet specified needs with appropriate consideration for public health and safety, cultural, societal, and environmental considerations.

SA3: Design solutions for **broadly- defined engineering technology problems and contribute to the design of systems,** components or processes to meet specified needs with appropriate consideration for public health and safety, cultural, societal, and environmental considerations.

WA4: Conduct investigations of *complex problems using research-based knowledge* and research methods including design of experiments, analysis and interpretation of data, and synthesis of information to provide valid conclusions.

SA4: Conduct investigations of **broadly-defined problems; locate, search and select relevant data from codes,** data bases and literature, design and conduct experiments to provide valid conclusions.

WA5: Create, select and apply appropriate techniques, resources, and modern engineering and IT tools, including prediction and modelling, to **complex engineering problems**, with an understanding of the limitations.

SA5: Select and apply appropriate techniques, resources, and modern engineering and IT tools, including prediction and modelling, to **broadly-defined engineering problems**, with an understanding of the limitations.

WA6: *Apply reasoning informed by contextual knowledge* to assess societal, health, safety, legal and cultural issues and the consequent responsibilities relevant to professional engineering practice and solutions to complex engineering problems.

SA6: **Demonstrate understanding** of the societal, health, safety, legal and cultural issues and the consequent responsibilities relevant to engineering technology practice and solutions to broadly defined engineering problems.

WA7: Understand and evaluate the sustainability and impact of *professional engineering work* in the solution of *complex engineering problems* in societal and environmental contexts.

SA7: Understand and evaluate the sustainability and impact of **engineering technology work** in the solution of **broadly defined engineering problems** in societal and environmental contexts.

WA8: *Apply ethical principles* and commit to professional ethics and responsibilities and norms of engineering practice.

SA8: **Understand and commit** to professional ethics and responsibilities and norms of engineering technology practice.

WA9: Function effectively as an individual, and as a member or leader in diverse teams and in multi-disciplinary settings.

SA9: Function effectively as an individual, and as a member or leader in diverse teams.

WA10: Communicate effectively on *complex engineering activities* with the engineering community and with society at large, such as being able to comprehend and write effective reports and design documentation, make effective presentations, and give and receive clear instructions.

SA10: Communicate effectively on **broadly-defined engineering activities** with the engineering community and with society at large, by being able to comprehend and write effective reports and design documentation, make effective presentations, and give and receive clear instructions

WA11: Demonstrate knowledge and understanding of engineering management principles and economic decision-making and apply these to *one's own work*, as a member and leader in a team, to manage projects and in multidisciplinary environments.

SA11: Demonstrate knowledge and understanding of engineering management principles and apply these to **one's own work**, as a member or leader in a team and to manage projects in multidisciplinary environments.

WA12: Recognize the need for, and have the preparation and ability to engage in independent and life-long learning in the *broadest context of technological change*.

SA12: Recognize the need for, and have the ability to engage in independent and life-long learning **in specialist technologies**.

In simple words the Bachelor level graduates should be able to solve complex engineering problems and a Diploma level graduate should be able to solve broadly defined problems in day to operations of the world of work related to engineering and technology.

It is obvious that when the POs shall be developed for Diploma level programs they shall be aligned with GAs written above with serial numbers from SA1 to SA12. Since the Diploma level graduates or '**Engineering Technologists**' as have been designated by International Engineering Alliance (IEC). The degree of complexity and difficulty levels of educational processes for Diploma graduates shall be much lower than the processes for bachelor level graduates.

6.3: TIPS TO RESPOND TO TYPICAL PORTIONS OF THE SAR EXCEPT ACCREDITATION CRITERIA.

In the part-II of SAR, **section II-7.1 & III-8**: *'Summary of budget for the CFY and the actual expenditure incurred in the CFYm1, CFYm2 and CFYm3 (for the department),* the department needs to give budget details for last 3(+1) years under the following budget heads. Some tips are provided to collect such information so that the budget data can be recreated, if not maintained properly.

i.   Laboratory equipment,
ii. Software,
iii. Laboratory consumable,
iv. Maintenance and spares,
v.   Research & development
vi. Training & Travel, and
vii. Miscellaneous expenses for academic activities

Laboratory equipment & consumables:

i.   Prepare a final list of equipment and appliances in each laboratory and check the entries in the permanent and consumable stock registers belonging to each laboratory.
ii. Collect the old records of purchase orders and bills of payment against the Lab equipment.
iii. In the *permanent stock register,* make entries related to every appliance/ equipment such as; name of the item, supplying vendor, bill details, date of receipt, cost, quantity, reference of main college stock register from where the item has been received, etc.
iv. In the consumable stock register, the entries of consumable items like materials, spare parts, electric wires and fittings, cost, and quantity. Mention in the remarks column where a particular item has been consumed or to whom it was issued with authorization of competent authority.
v.   All the stock registers should be registered with the stock registers' list and duly signed by the registrar and the director of the institute for

the purpose of authenticity of the record. Each register should mention the total number of pages in each register.

vi. The budgeted expenditure in a financial year of the department can be worked out on the basis of the total expenditure, by collating all the expenses incurred on all the laboratories, on non-consumable and consumable items acquired in each financial year with 10 to 15% enhancement to take care of expenses on missed items.

For all the budget heads the department should create an authentic record and maintain with adequate safety and security.

6.4: TIPS FOR PREPARING TYPICAL RECORD FILES RELATED TO INSTITUTE AND PROGRAM

SAR-Part-III: List of Record files (Required for all levels of Engg. & technology programs)

List of Documents / Records to be made available during the Visit of the team of experts appointed by NBA.

(Records of three years to be made available, wherever applicable)

The list below is just a guideline. The Institution may prepare their own list of documents in support of the SAR that they are submitting. The soft copy of these documents in the form of statements and list only may be appended with SAR..

The lists of following files have already given in the chapter 5 under section 5.5.

- **Institute Specific Record Files = 17 files**
- **Program Specific Record Files = 32 files**
- **Program specific academic exhibits = 14 files**

Some tips & examples related a few typical record files

File # I.2: Examples of documents for keeping records of meetings and resolutions

Document-1: Circular cum Agenda of meetings of Board of Governors (BoG).

PQ COLLEGE SCIENCE AND TECHNOLOGY, BHARATNAGAR

No- BoG/Agenda Note/ 20ZZ/ Date- X/Y/20ZZ

Circular with Agenda Note:

For agenda issue P of ***7th meeting*** of the Board of Governors to be held on X /Y/20ZZ from 10 AM in the Seminar Hall 02.

Agenda Issue P: To Approve Institutional Development Plan (IDP) of PQCST, Bharatnagar for submitting to MHRD-GoI, NPIU, Noida through DTE-RS & SPFU-RS, on S/T/20ZZ for obtaining funding under the World Bank assisted Project TEQIP-II.

Agenda Issue Q: to empower the chairman to take appropriate & prompt decisions in the best interest of PQCST -Group, Bharatnagar and for ensuring smooth implementation of the TEQIP-II Project. The chairman shall submit action taken report in subsequent BoG meetings for the purpose of ratification of the decisions taken.

Background Information:

- GoI, MHRD, through implementing agency NPIU, Noida had launched a 15 year Project of Quality Improvement of Technical Education Program (TEQIP). TEQIP's first five year phase was completed in year 2009 and currently its second 4 year phase has been recently launched for a period 2011-12 till 2014-15 under the title of TEQIP-II.
- PQCST was found eligible for funding under TEQIP-II during 20ZZ and SPFU, DTE on have asked us to prepare and submit our IDP latest by for considering our selection under competition with other institutes of India. At National level only 20 private unaided technical

institutes will be selected and this selection is definitely going to be quite tough. However, PQCST has very bright chances from the state.

• This IDP implies funding of Rs 400 lacs with the following major aspects of reforms implied in the IDP;

    o   The foci of the project are (i) improving the learning outcomes of the Engineering UG / PG pass-outs of PQRST, and (ii) improving the employability of the pass-outs of PQRST.

    o   PQCST shall become an Autonomous Institute within two years as a consequence of 100% Academic Autonomy given by the university. PQCST shall make its own curricula and conduct examination. Perhaps the marks sheets and Degrees will be jointly awarded to pass outs by the affiliating University and PQCST. The Director will submit a detailed document to BoG for approval which shall define the implications and responsibilities of functionaries relate to implementation of academic autonomy. A curriculum development center and Examination Center shall be established for smooth implementation of the autonomy.

    o   PQCST will need to open four separate accounts in a commercial bank with deposits equal to 1% of IRG from Students' fee contributed in each account every year for first four years. These funds will be known as Faculty Development fund, Equipment replacement fund, maintenance fund and corpus fund. These funds will be used to sustain the benefits and reforms caused by the TEQIP-II project.

    o   The major investment shall be done on establishing and up grading existing PG Labs and library resources and developing faculty members through Short term and long term training / education programs. However, other managerial, financial and Administrative officers will also be sent for special training programs.

    o   Many academic and non-academic reforms and targets to be achieved are implied in the project which have been detailed out in various sections and action plans given in the IDP.

- The blanket approval of the IDP and empowerment of the chairman to take decisions as and when required in the best interest of PQCST. The project shall help PQCST in general in smooth implementation of the project activities. However, the chairman shall keep on submitting the action taken report to the BoG in the subsequent meetings for ratification purposes.

Director, Secretary PQCST   Date X/Y/20ZZ

Copy with compliments to honorable members of the PQCST, Bhopal:

1

2

3 ......   Date X/Y/20ZZ

Director Secretary

,,,,,,,,,,,,,,,,,,,,,,,,,,,,,,,..................................,,,,,,,,,,,,,,,,,,,,,,,,,,,,,,,,.............

Document-2: Suggested format of minutes of BoG Meeting

PQ COLLEGE SCIENCE AND TECHNOLOGY, BHARATNAGAR

Subject: Minutes of *twenty seventh meeting* of the Board of Governors held on x/y/yyzz from 2.00 PM in the Seminar Hall 02.

Meeting attended by: Chairman, Vice-chairman, & Members: 1, 2, 3, 5, 6, 7, 8, 9 & Director/ Secretary

The meeting started at 02:30 pm and the secretary presented each issue in the agenda for discussion and / or approval by the members.

Agenda issue A1:   To constitute **INSTITUTIONAL TEQIP (implementation) UNIT (ITU), commensurate with the Format given in Project Implementation**

Plan (PIP) 2009: ANNEX- IV (B).a, (ii) (format for making IDP)

The secretary recalled the details of the TEQIP-II project and its academic benefits to PQCST. He explained the requirements of ITU for smooth implementation of TEQIP. The following persons were nominated for different positions of PQCST-ITU: 1ˢᵗ person shall be the coordinator.

1.   2.   3.   4.   5.

Resolution 27.01-   **The BoG members approved the members of the PQCST -ITU as above.**

Agenda Issue B: To **review** the **BoG structure** commensurate with the **norms of UGC** and fulfill the requirements of TEQIP (PIP p 78, Annexure – I, p 138, PIP- p 184, Clause 2.1-5)

The secretary presented the implications of applying for TEQIP-II project. The members were of the view that the PQCST is regulated by AICTE. How, for one project the BoG structure can be amended which is commensurate with a non-regulating body like UGC. It was suggested that the matter should be postponed for gathering more information & guidance from SPFU/ DTE/ AICTE.

Resolution 27.02: The issue will be taken up in the next meeting with more supporting information

The meeting was finished with vote of thanks to the Chairman of the BoG.

Director / Secretary   Date:

NB: Registrar to circulate the minutes to all the members

To Registrar: Please circulate the Circular & Agenda Note to all the members for the 7ᵀᴴ BOG meeting in Chairman's chamber

P.26. Rubrics developed to validate the POs.

Developing and executing direct, indirect methods and rubrics to develop & evaluate PO's (Program Outcomes).

NBA's POs' which are aligned with GAs' of Washington Accord shall be assessed using following guidelines or rubrics for a BE program. If we assume that the difficulty level of acquisition of POs of BE levels is 100% than the DL levels for diploma program should be of much lower levels as suggested in the following guidelines.

1. **Engineering Knowledge:** Apply knowledge of mathematics, science, engineering fundamentals and an engineering specialization to the solution of Numerical Engg Problems (Q=40-50 per subject), and Complex engineering problems. (Q=10 per subject)

   - **Closed end Numerical Problems:** (DL or Difficulty Level: 45%-50%)
   More Tutorial classes and home work in medium (7-15) self-help groups of students.
   - **Closed ended complex problems: (DL= 50–60%)**
   Give application type multi subjects related numerical problems to solve in smaller groups of 5 to 9 persons
   - **Open Ended Complex Engg Problems (DL= 60-70%)**
   Create a question bank with the help of industries and commerce and let the students take such problems as micro projects within every subject. Students take such subject based micro-projects & submit solutions in small groups of 3 to 4 students

2. **Problem Analysis:** Identify, formulate, research literature and analyze complex engineering problems reaching substantiated conclusions using first principles of mathematics, natural sciences and engineering sciences. **(Q= DL 60-70%, 1 per subject), (Q= DL 70-75%, 1 per subject)**

   Develop a question bank of open ended multi –subject based complex problems.

Problem Analysis DL = 60 -70%: Identify problems during industrial visits. Undertake its analysis in smaller groups of 5 to 10 persons. Present a seminar and submit as tutorial work.

Problem Analysis DL = 70 -75%: Identify problems during industrial training. Undertake its analysis in smaller groups of 3 to 5 persons as micro projects. Present a seminar and submit. Introduce use of ISO and BIS standards in problem solving assignments

3. **Conduct investigations** of complex engineering problems using research-based knowledge and research methods including design of experiments, analysis and interpretation of data and synthesis of information to provide valid conclusions.

   - Introduce such micro projects as Lab assignments to investigate;
   - Verify given Properties of materials
   - Verify Properties/ specifications of some appliances and systems
   - Investigate in to maintenance, quality and reliability issues of some equipment recently procured.
   - DL= 60-70% at least one in each lab in a semester
   - Introduce use of ISO and BIS standards in problem solving assignments

4. **Modern Tool Usage:** Create, select and apply appropriate techniques, resources and modern engineering and IT tools including prediction and modeling to complex engineering activities with an understanding of the limitations.

   - Mechanical Engg *Simulation-X tools* like suggested in: http://www.itisim.com/simulationx/ for Mechanics, Power Transmissions, Dynamic Analysis of Automobile systems, Use of *CAM and CADD* for minor and Major Projects' problem solving
   - http://electronics-engineering-software.fyxm.net/
   - http://www.engineeringtoolbox.com/
   - http://linux.softpedia.com/get/Adaptive-Technologies/
   - http://www.galilmc.com/learning/tutorials.php, http://www.everythingrf.com

5. **The Engineer and Society**: Apply reasoning informed by contextual knowledge to assess societal, health, safety, legal and cultural issues and the consequent responsibilities relevant to professional engineering practice.

- We need to subscribe for a generous number of good magazines and science and technology research journals in our library and give some time to students for visiting and reading at Library.
- The better ways of doing this is to have departmental seminars once in a fortnight through students' chapter of the dept. Give themes from the articles of the library resources. This will improve their search skills, reading, writing, presenting and arguing skills etc.
- Some awards for best theme papers & seminar presentation can do wonders.

6. **Environment and Sustainability:** Understand the impact of professional engineering solutions in societal and environmental contexts and demonstrate knowledge of and need for sustainable development.

- Introduce relevant case studies focusing on adverse consequences on environment due to faulty designs which did not take into account the impact of adverse effects their products or processes on environment and on society.
- The teaching of environmental sciences should include to subject of visits to the typical site and locations where such adverse effects have created visible damages to the environment and society. Suitable video programs and episodes from Discovery channels can also be used to supplement such studies.
- Use of Visual Viva is recommended for such subjects

7. **Ethics:** Apply ethical principles and commit to professional ethics and responsibilities and norms of engineering practice.

- Public health and safety, quality, usefulness, efficiency, cost/risk/benefit analysis, truthfulness, trustworthiness, loyalty, meeting targets of time, And to encourage students to take ethical responsibility seriously. Teaching engineering ethics can increase student knowledge of relevant standards, especially the consequences of departing from them. For example, part of teaching students to take operating costs into account when designing something is pointing out how uneconomical the design is if they don't. The classroom and laboratory provide a safe place to make mistakes and learn from them—ethical mistakes as well as purely technical ones.

- o http://environmental.org.uk/uploads/downloads/Engineering_ethics_in_practice.pdf
- o http://www.engineersaustralia.org.au/sites/default/files/shado/About%20Us/Overview/Governance/CodeOfEthics2000.pdf
- o http://www.engineersaustralia.org.au/sites/default/files/shado/About%20Us/Overview/Governance/CodeOfEthics2000.pdf
- o http://www.nspe.org/Ethics/EthicsResources/Otherresources/appliedethics.html
- o http://www.onlineethics.org/?gclid=CJmR0KDh87MCFch66wodlXEAuA

- There is widespread agreement that the best way to teach professional ethics can be done by using stories, drama & cases.

8. **Individual and Team Work:** Function effectively as an individual, and as a member or leader in diverse teams and in multi-disciplinary settings.

- Micro/ Minor projects as problem solving teams and working in groups during extracurricular activities, Technology- festivals, Engg-Exhibitions, seminars and Lab work are excellent opportunities to learn to Live together and work together. Become leader and active members of a problem solving team.
- Self-development, individual library assignments, home-work, debating etc. are opportunities to groom the own personality in competition with others.

- However, in both the cases, Faculty's greatest contribution shall come in the form of orienting students and assessing their team work performance against declared criteria and its indicators.

9. **Communication**: Communicate effectively on complex engineering activities with the engineering community and with society at large, such as being able to comprehend and write effective reports and design documentation, make effective presentations and give and receive clear instructions.

- http://www.ehow.com/how_8484370_teach-adults-communication-skills.html
- http://www.seenmagazine.us/articles/article-detail/articleid/209/teaching-basic-communication-skills.aspx
- http://www.ask.co.uk/how/how_can_i_teach_adults_communication_skills
- http://www.communicationpractices.org/

Identify weaknesses in Communication sub-skills: reading/ writing, speaking / listening, Making Visuals/ interpreting visuals, creating body language cues/ interpreting body cues etc. are the pairs that are learnt as basic skills in family and in schools.
Such skills can be supplemented by integrating them with day to day teaching -learning work undertaken by students in Classrooms, labs, projects, industrial training and extracurricular activities. Make students aware of assessment criteria for grading these sub-skills along with the technology content being learnt.

10. **Project Management and Finance:** Demonstrate knowledge and understanding of engineering and management principles and apply these to one's own work, as a member and leader in a team, to manage projects and in multidisciplinary environments.

- The graduation major project experience gives a great opportunity to facilitate learning of these skills. Major project is offered during 4th Year. Major Project's experience should be designed very carefully involving participation of experts from industry to bring in the factor of reality, panel of experienced senior professors from different disciplines to bring in variety of aspects of Inter-disciplinary Engg Practices and standards (ISO/ BIS).

- The whole batch of students should be transformed in cohesive teams of 5 to 7 students by students' choice to the extent possible.
- A number of Project problems with its synapsis should be pooled by faculty, experts and students as an ongoing process on the academic website of the Dept. The selection of the 2 /3 project problems should be done by the leader of the team who should present after presentation of seminar on the proposed strategies of solving all the three problems.
- The final major project selection should be defended on the bases of declared criteria and be allocated by a select committee.
- A guideline document should be followed by all the teams to complete the project work with intermediate progress monitoring meetings with faculty guides.

11. **Life-long Learning:** Recognize the need for and have the preparation and ability to engage in independent and life- long learning in the broadest context of technological change.

- Students are encouraged to read a number of published (physical & digital) materials as a routine practice for doing different kinds of learning assignments. If the faculty is good life-long learners then and only then they can induce life learning attitudes in the students.
- To nurture self-learning and continuous experience dissemination to knowledge society in and around the campus, some small investment shall be required to publish digital work of students & faculty on it's the institute's intranet.

Some rubric which shall be assessing sub-skills implied in the POs should be assessed by using rubrics comparable to unique level and multi-level rating scales rating scales.

Prepare to answer questions which may be asked by NBA's Inspection team

All such questions are also given in chapter 5 which should be carefully prepared before the visit of NBA team

CHAPTER 7.0

NBA ACCREDITATION OF PG TECHNICAL PROGRAMS

7.1: Tips for Creating a SAR for ME & M Tech Programs
7.2: Tips for Creating a SAR for MCA Programs
7.3: Tips for Creating a SAR for MBA Programs for T-II institutions

7.1: TIPS FOR CREATING A SAR FOR ME & M TECH PROGRAMS

The criteria of Tier-I & Tier-II for PG programs in Engg. & Technology are the similar to the criteria for accreditation of Bachelor of Engg & technology programs. The question arises then how one can differentiate between the graduates of Bachelor and PG level programs in Engg & Tech. This understanding shall be helpful in preparing the PEOs and POs at PG level accreditation. The criteria are slightly different for tier-I (autonomous) and Tier-II (non-autonomous) PG programs.

# Criteria for ME/ M Tech Points	Maximum & Minimum	
Class of Institution	T-I	T-II
1. *Vision, Mission & PEOs*	*75 & 45*	*75 & 45*
2. **Program outcomes**	**250 & 150**	**225 & 135**
3. *Program Curriculum*	*75 & 45*	*75 & 45*
4. **Students' Performance**	**100 & 60**	**100 & 60**
5. **Faculty Contributions**	**200 & 120**	**100 & 60**
6. Facilities and Technical Support	75 & 45	75 & 45
7. ***Teaching-Learning processes***	***75 & 45***	***75 & 45***
8. Governance, Institutional Support and Financial Resources	75 & 45	75 & 4
9. Continuous Improvement	75 & 45	100 & 60
• Total score (For Tier-I)	1000 & 600	

- Total score (for Tier- II):
  - o Under T-I, if the score is more than 750 with minimum of 60% in mandatory criteria 1 & 4 to 8, accreditation is awarded for 5 years. Whereas a program under T-I, which shall score a minimum of 600 points in aggregate (without any stipulation), will be eligible for the status of prospective candidate for accreditation under T-I.
  - o Under T-II, if the score is between 600 & 750 with 60% score in mandatory criteria 1 & 4 to 8, accreditation is awarded for 2 years. If the scoring a minimum of 750 points in aggregate out of 1000 points with minimum score of 60% in mandatory fields (Cr-1 and Cr 4 to 8) shall be eligible for accreditation for 5 years. The same criteria shall be applicable for provisional accreditation of new programs.

After going through the table of criteria provided above, the following observations should establish how the weights of different criteria are in variations with those meant for UG programs.

- The Criteria 1 & 3 related to PEOs and Program Curriculum respectively are given relatively less weights as compared to criteria for UG programs.
- The Criteria 2, 4 & 5 related to **program outcomes**, students' performance & **faculty contributions** respectively together have been

given more weight of the order of 55%, therefore the SAR should stress on these three criteria which implies:

o   Use new methodologies and research facilitating environment where highly qualified faculty contribute in teaching learning along with research & development activities, indirect assessment techniques and rubrics assess directly and indirectly the performance of both students and faculty and encourage them to indulge in innovation and pursuing new knowledge during studies and during their rest of active life.

o   The faculty and scholars both should contribute more in the area of research & development related problem solving.

o   In view of this, the GAs of PG scholars have been changed adequately to accommodate the R&D skills. These GAs are described below.

Graduate Attributes (GAs) of PG scholars as per NBA's Manual for PG (version Jan 2013)

1. **Scholarship of Knowledge**: Acquire in-depth knowledge of specific discipline or professional area, including wider and global perspective, with an ability to discriminate, evaluate, analyze and synthesize existing and new knowledge, and integration of the same for enhancement of knowledge.

2. **Critical Thinking:** Analyze complex engineering problems critically, apply independent judgment for synthesizing information to make intellectual and/or creative advances for conducting research in a wider theoretical, practical and policy context.

3. **Problem Solving:** Think laterally and originally, conceptualize and solve engineering problems, evaluate a wide range of potential solutions for those problems and arrive at feasible, optimal solutions and environmental factors considering public health and safety, cultural, societal environmental factors in the core areas of expertise.

4. **Research skill:** Extract information pertinent to unfamiliar problems through literature survey and experiments, analyze and interpret data, demonstrate higher order skill and view things in a broader perspective,

contribute individually? In group(s) to the development of scientific/ technological knowledge in one or more domain of engineering.

5. **Usage of modern tools**: Create, select, learn, and apply appropriate techniques, resources, and modern engineering and IT tools, including prediction and modelling, to complex engineering activities with understanding of the limitations.

6. **Collaborative and Multidisciplinary work**: Possess knowledge and understanding of group dynamics, recognize opportunities and contribute positively to collaborative-multidisciplinary scientific research demonstrate a capacity for self-management and team work, decision-making based on open-mindedness, objectivity and rational analysis in order to achieve common goals and further the learning of themselves as well as others.

7. **Project Management and Finance**: Demonstrate knowledge and understanding of engineering and management principles and apply the same to one's own work, as a member and leader in a team, manage projects efficiently in respective disciplines and multidisciplinary environments after consideration of economic and financial factors.

8. **Communication**: Communicate with the engineering community, and society at large, regarding complex engineering activities confidently and effectively, such as, being able to comprehend and write effective reports and design documentation by adhering to appropriate standards, make effective presentations, and give and receive clear instructions.

9. **Life-long Learning**: recognize the need for, and have the preparation and ability to engage in life-long learning independently, with a high level of enthusiasm and commitment to improve knowledge and competence continuously.

10. **Ethical Practices and Social Responsibility**: Acquire professional and intellectual integrity, professional code of conduct, ethics of research and scholarship, consideration of the impact of research outcomes on professional practices and an understanding of responsibility to contribute to the community for sustainable development of society.

11. **Independent and reflective Learning**: Observe and examine critically the outcome of one's actions and make corrective measures

subsequently, and learn from mistakes without depending on external feedback.

Thus the POs for a PG program shall be formulated in alignment with the GAs described above. The infrastructure and facilities in the PG labs should be capable & conducive of conducting & publishing research to inform engineering community to nurture the economy and happiness of the citizens of the country and globe at large.

As the POs content is different, therefore the methodology of teaching and self-study assignments shall have more focus of developing problem solving skill along with abilities of pursuing research and development projects.

7.2: TIPS FOR CREATING A SAR FOR MCA PROGRAM

#	Criteria for MCA	Marks Maximum & Minimum	
		T-I	T-II
1.	Vision, Mission & PEOs	75 & 45	75
2.	Program outcomes	175 & 105	150
3.	Program Curriculum	75 & 75	100
4.	Students' Performance	100 & 60	100 & 60
5.	Faculty Contributions	175 & 105	175 & 105
6.	Facilities and Technical Support	100 & 60	100 & 60
7.	Academic support & T-L process	75 & 45	125 & 75
8.	Governance, Institutional Support and Financial Resources	75 & 45	75 & 45
9.	Continuous Improvement	100 & 60	100
•	Total score (For Tier-I)	1000 & 600	
•	Total score (for Tier- II):		

o Under T-I, if the score is more than 750 with minimum of 60% in mandatory criteria 4 to 8, accreditation is awarded for 5 years. Whereas a program under T-I, which shall score a minimum of 600 points in aggregate (without any stipulation), will be eligible for the status of prospective candidate for accreditation under T-I.

o   Under T-II, if the score is between 600 & 750 with 60% score in mandatory criteria 1 & 4 to 8, accreditation is awarded for 2 years. If the scoring a minimum of 750 points in aggregate out of 1000 points with minimum score of 60% in mandatory fields (Cr-1 and Cr 4 to 8) shall be eligible for accreditation for 5 years. The same criteria shall be applicable for provisional accreditation of new programs.

- When we compare the weights allocated to different criteria to BE program for T-I (4 years UG) and MCA program for T-I (3 years PG), then we shall find that the weights of first three criteria are marginally lesser and weights of criteria 4 & 6 are slightly more. It implies that the management of MCA program should care more for students' performance and support facilities as compared to the care related to PEOs, POs and Curriculum.

- After looking at the table of criteria the criteria 2, 4 5 & 6 have been given more importance, it means that the Performance of students and faculty have to be monitored & developed more critically than other criteria for seeking accreditation for 5 years. It is also essential that the technical support and facilities should be quite rich so that the students and faculty can contribute substantially without much hurdles.

- When we compare weights of T-I and T-II then it is quite obvious that the non-autonomous institutions applying for NBA Accreditation under T-II category, should bother more for technical facilities and T-L processes as compared to T-I institutions.

7.3: TIPS FOR CREATING A SAR FOR MBA PROGRAM FOR T-II INSTITUTIONS

Business school evaluation sheet {Ref: SAR Business school, Nov 2012}

SNo   Criteria   Max points

1.0 **Organization Mission, Governance and Leadership**   **120**

2.0 **Input (Enablers)   360**

    2.1 - Students 35
    2.2 - Faculty 50
    2.3 - Physical Infra-structure 40
    2.4 - IT Infrastructure 50
    2.5 – Library 55
    2.6 – Global Input 35
    2.7 – Quality Assurance Policy 40
    2.8 – Finance 55

3.0 **Processes**   **360**

    3.1 Academic Assessment Process 100
    3.2 Placement Process 40
    3.3 R&D Process 45
    3.4 Leadership & Governance 20
    3.5 MDPs, Consultancy Process and Promotion Policy 75
    3.6 Faculty, Faculty Appraisal and Promotion Policy 40
    3.7 Internalization Process 20
    3.8 Staff Appraisal, Development and Promotion Process 20

4.0 Outcome (**Results**)   **360**

    4.1 academic Results 55
    4.2 Placement 60
    4.3 Entrepreneurship and Job Creation 10

4.4 Value and Ethic centric Outcomes 25

4.5 Industry Interaction

4.6 MDPs 36

4.7 International / Global 24

4.8 Research and Innovation 30

4.9 Stakeholders' Satisfaction 40

4.10 Contribution to society 25

Total   **1200**

Detailed guidelines have been provided in the Evaluation document and SAR format to enable you to interpret the criteria and you can easily prepare the SAR document. However, if you consult some experienced retired professor the quality of your document shall be far better than what you alone can do. However, you should carefully the tips given under **prerequisites** & **ACCREDITATION Status decision making** before starting your SAR filling.

A: **PRE-REQUISITES**:

Following are the pre-requisites which must be satisfied by an institution prior to application for accreditation of the management program [MBA] in a department:

1. At least two batches of the Management Program [MBA] must have graduated.
2. At least 33% of the faculty associated with the Management Program [MBA] should have a Ph.D. Degree, and the remaining should have a Master's Degree in the related areas.
3. For a batch of 120 students, the minimum number of faculty in the Management Program [MBA] should not be less than 8.

B: **ACCREDITATION Status decision making**:

1. The program gets the status *'Accredited'* for the next **5 years**, beginning from the date of issue of the letter from NBA, provided it

has a minimum score of 900 points, and scores minimum qualifying 60% marks in each of the criterion specified.

2. The program gets the status *'Provisionally Accredited'* for the next **2 years**, beginning from the date of issue of the letter from NBA, provided it has a minimum score of 720 points, and scores minimum qualifying 45% marks in each of the criterion specified. An institution may also apply for up-gradation to *'Full Accreditation'* of the program after overcoming the weaknesses/ deficiencies.

3. If a program scores less than 720 points, it is given the status of *'Not Accredited'*.

It is highly desirable that the department conducts a deep SWOT analysis of the program as well as the institute before initiating the documentation of SAR. The program coordinator should have more than five years of experience for enabling him/her to understand the educational processes as well as the meaning of the terms used in the accreditation SAR.

QUALITY ASSURANCE ACCREDITATION OF INSTITUTIONS BY NAAC

8.1: Rationale

8.2: NAAC Accreditation criteria

8:1 RATIONALE

National Assessment & Accreditation Council was established on 16 September 1994 (**NAAC**: http://www.naac.gov.in), under UGC Act of 1956(3)- section 12CCC in accordance with the National Education Policy & the Plan of Action (POA-1992) of Govt. of India with its head-quarters at Bangalore, Karnataka State, India. *Its **vision** is 'to make quality the defining element of higher education in India through a combination of self and external quality evaluation, promotion and sustenance initiatives.' And its **mission** are; 1. To arrange for periodic assessment and accreditation of institutions of higher education or units thereof, or specific academic programs or projects; 2. To stimulate the academic environment for promotion of quality of teaching-learning and research in higher education institutions; 3. To encourage self-evaluation, accountability, autonomy and innovations in higher education; 4. To undertake quality-related research studies, consultancy and training programs, and 5. To collaborate with other stakeholders of higher education for quality evaluation,* *promotion and sustenance*. Recently the value frame work has also been added which is given below. **Value Framework**: *To promote the following core values among the HEIs of the country: 1. Contribution to National Development, 2. Fostering Global Competencies among Students. 3. Inculcating a Value System among Students 4. Promoting the Use of Technology, 5. Quest for Excellence*

Guided by its vision and striving to achieve its mission, the NAAC primarily assesses the quality of institutions of higher education that volunteer for the process, through an internationally accepted methodology. However, as per circular issued in 2014, the Universities and institutions should undergo NAAC accreditation in order to receive the benefits of UGC grants for the academic developmental activities of the institutions. As a result of this circular, many colleges and universities which were not intending to acquire NAAC accreditation are motivated to apply to NAAC and are in queue for receiving accreditation certificates/ status. A bill - National Accreditation Regulatory Authority for Higher Educational Institutions Bill, 2010 has been introduced in Parliament of India to make it mandatory for every higher educational institution in the country (other than institutions engaged in agricultural education) to be accredited by an independent accreditation agency. However, the bill is still pending for serious attention of the MPs of India.

Recently, NAAC has been awarded financial support of Rs 170 million during year 2013-14, under the project of MHRD, GoI, under *Rashtriya Ucchatar Shiksha Abhiyan* **(RUSA)** Project and UGC's proposal under its proposed scheme titled as National Quality Renaissance Initiative (NQRI). The major features of NQRI are

i.   Awareness building, popularization and promotion of Quality Assurance Mentoring to Higher Education Institutions,

ii.   Building Collegium of Assessors and

iii.   Quality Sustenance and Enhancement Initiatives.

The awareness about the need of quality assurance and accreditation certification is increasing with time although slowly but steadily. There are economic reasons as well which are pressing hard many institutions to improve their performances for attracting more number of talented students with higher paying capacities. They have understood that quality assurance not only shall enable them to survive but also shall lead them from the current loss making status to a profit making status in future. Some of the ambitious and forward looking institutions are under taking accreditation from International bodies such as International Accreditation Organization (IAO) and ABET (the Accreditation Board of Engineering and Technology" of USA http://www.abet.org). These institutions hope to expand their operations in foreign countries in addition to getting students from nearby countries and become more reputed and profitable enterprises. Their hope is also justifiable as well as achievable.

Recently in 2013, commensurate with the Supreme Court of India's judgment, the power of approval of new Engg Programs or any other issue related to their extension etc. has been transferred to the affiliating University (State or Center owned) in whose jurisdiction the college is or shall be located. These universities shall also compel these colleges to install minimum quality assurance by observing the UGC's approval norms in true spirit. Thus as per order of the of the UGC of india, **every professional technical college needs to undertake both NAAC Accreditation as a well performing Institute and NBA Accreditation for each professional program being offered by it ensuring proper placement and global mobility of graduates.**

8.2: NAAC ACCREDITATION APPROACH

As per NAAC the term Assessment and Accreditation is broadly used for understanding the "Quality Status" of an institution. This is expressed in terms of Grade values like **A, B & C** for accredited institutions and **D** for not accredited institutions. In the context of Higher Education, the accreditation status indicates that the particular Higher Educational Institutions (HEI) –a College, a University, or any other recognized Unit therein, meets the standards of quality as set by the NAAC or any other accreditation agency, in terms of its performance, as assessed on the bases of the quality criteria such as: the educational processes and outcomes, covering the curriculum, teaching-learning, evaluation, faculty, research, infrastructure, learning resources, organization, governance, financial well-being and student services.

NAAC follows the process of Grade accreditation only and does not undertake threshold accreditation, that is, the Grade is only a relative value assigned to a university and does not denote an absolute attribute of quality.

Under the new methodology introduced by NAAC with effect from 1st April, 2007, the higher education institutions are assessed and accredited by a two-step approach.

- In the first step, the institution is required to seek 'Institutional Eligibility for Quality Assessment (IEQA)' and
- the second step is the assessment and accreditation of the institute under the grades 'A', 'B', 'C' for accredited institutions, and 'D' for those not accredited

NAAC has developed different manuals for Universities, Affiliated Colleges and Autonomous Colleges taking into cognizance their specific roles and attributes. The manuals are comprehensive and user friendly, providing information on how the **self-study report (SSR)** is to be prepared, the criteria and key aspects to be addressed and the style of presentation.

Henceforth, the **SSRs** for Universities, Affiliated Colleges and Autonomous Colleges, may be presented in one document. The total number of pages excluding the department-wise inputs should not exceed 200 pages. It may comprise of the following sections:

- Preface
- Executive Summary inclusive of the SWOC (Strengths, Weaknesses, Opportunities and Challenges) analysis of the institution
- Profile of the Institution
- Evaluative Report - Criteria-wise
- Evaluative Report - Department-wise

These manuals (version 2012) are available for the following categories of institutions

i. Universities
ii. Affiliated/ constituent colleges
iii. Affiliated Colleges
iv. Teacher Education institutions
v. Physical Education Institutions

vi. Health Science Institutions

vii. Academic Staff Colleges

NAAC assessment lays focus on the institutional developments with reference to three aspects: *Quality initiative, Quality sustenance and Quality enhancement.* The overall quality assurance framework of NAAC thus focuses on the values and desirable practices of Higher Education Institutions (HEIs) and incorporates the core elements of quality assurance i.e. internal and external assessment for continuous improvement.

NAAC's "manuals for self-study" maps out different inputs, processes and outputs and facilitates HEIs to evaluate their strengths, weaknesses and areas for improvement. The self-evaluation process and the subsequent preparation of the Self-Study Report (SSR) to be submitted to NAAC involves the participation of all the stakeholders – management, faculty members, administrative staff, students, parents, employers, community and alumni. While the participation of internal stakeholders i.e. management, staff and students provide credibility and ownership to the activity and could lead to newer initiatives, interaction with the external stakeholders facilitate the development process of the institution and their educational services. Overall it is expected to serve as a catalyst for institutional self-improvement, promote innovation and *strengthen the urge to excel.*

Till July 8, 2013, a total of 179 universities and 5156 colleges had been accredited by NAAC.

The qualitative part of the outcome of assessment & accreditation process is called the **Peer Team Report (PTR).** The quantitative report prepared by the team highlighting its judgments. The quantitative part of the outcome comprises the criterion-wise quality assessment, resulting in the final *cumulative grade point average (CGPA).* A letter grade and a performance descriptor for CGPA between 3.01-4.00, is accredited as **A** (very good), 2.01-3.00 is accredited as **B** (good), 1.51-2.00 is accredited as **C** (satisfactory) and below or equal to 1.50 is accredited as **D** (unsatisfactory). Institutions getting grade 'D' are intimated and notified as *'Assessed and found not qualified for accreditation'*

8.3: NAAC ACCREDITATION CRITERIA

NAAC identifies seven criteria for accreditation:

1. Curricular aspects,
2. Teaching-learning and evaluation,
3. Research, Consultancy and extension,
4. Infrastructure and learning resources,
5. Student support and progression,
6. Governance and leadership and Management
7. Innovations and best practices

The Key Aspects identified under each of the seven criteria reflect the processes and values of the HEI on which assessment is made. The questions under each of the Key Aspects focus in particular on the outcomes, the institutional provisions which contribute to these and their impact on student learning and development.

The strengths or weaknesses in one area may have an effect on quality in another area. Thus the issues addressed within the Criteria and Key Aspects are closely inter-related and may appear to be overlapping. The criteria and the Key Aspects are not a set of standards or measurement tools by themselves and do not cover everything which happens in every HEI. They are the levers for transformational change and provide 9 an external point of reference for evaluating the quality of the institution under assessment.

NAAC uses the same framework across the country. Using the same framework across the country provides a common language about quality and makes it much easier for everyone to go in one direction and in evidence based policy making.

Cr. 1. Curricular Aspects

The criterion looks into how the curriculum either assigned by a University or marginally supplemented or enriched by an institution, or totally remade, depending on the freedom allowed in curricular design, aligns with the institutional mission. It also considers the practices of an institution in initiating a wide range of program options and courses that are in tune with the emerging national and global trends and relevant to the local needs.

Key aspects

1   Curriculum Design and Development *(For* Universities *and Autonomous Colleges) or*

1.1 Curriculum Planning and Implementation *(For Affiliated/Constituent Colleges)*

1.2 Academic flexibility

1.3 Curriculum Enrichment

1.4 Feedback System

Cr. 2. Teaching-Learning and Evaluation

This criterion deals with the efforts of an institution to serve students of different backgrounds and abilities, through effective teaching-learning experiences. Interactive instructional techniques that engage students in higher order 'thinking' and investigation, through the use of interviews, focused group discussions, debates, projects, presentations, experiments, practicum, internship and application of ICT resources, are important considerations. It also probes into the adequacy, competence as well as the continuous professional development of the faculty who handle the programs of study.

Key Aspects

2.1 Student Enrolment and Profile

2.2 Catering to Student Diversity

2.3 Teaching-Learning Process

2.4 Teacher Quality

2.5 Evaluation Process and Reforms

2.6 Student Performance and Learning Outcomes

Cr. 3. Research, Consultancy and Extension

This criterion seeks information on the policies, practices and outcomes of the institution, with reference to research, consultancy and extension. It deals with the facilities provided and efforts made by the institution to promote a 'research culture'.

Key Aspects

3.1 Promotion of Research
3.2 Resource Mobilization for Research
3.3 Research Facilities
3.4 Research Publications and Awards
3.5 Consultancy
3.6 Extension Activities and Institutional Social Responsibility
3.7 Collaborations

Cr. 4. Infrastructure and Learning Resources

This criterion attempts to illustrate data on the adequacy and optimal use of the facilities available in an institution to maintain the quality of academic and other programs on the campus. It also requires information on how every constituent of the institution - students, teachers and staff - benefit from these facilities.

Key Aspects

4.1 Physical Facilities
4.2 Library as a Learning Resource
4.3 IT Infrastructure
4.4 Maintenance of Campus Facilities

Cr. 5. Student Support and Progression

The highlights of this criterion are the efforts of an institution to provide necessary assistance to students, to acquire meaningful experiences for learning at the campus and to facilitate their holistic development and progression.

Key Aspects

5.1 Student Mentoring and Support
5.2 Student Progression
5.3 Student Participation and Activities

Cr. 6. Governance, Leadership and Management

This criterion helps gather data on the policies and practices of an institution in the matter of planning human resources, recruitment, training, performance appraisal, financial management and the overall role of leadership in institution building.

Key Aspects

6.1 Institutional Vision and Leadership
6.2 Strategy Development and Deployment
6.3 Faculty Empowerment Strategies
6.4 Financial Management and Resource Mobilization
6.5 Internal Quality Assurance System (IQAS)

Cr. 7. Innovations and Best Practices

This criterion focuses on the innovative efforts of an institution that help in its academic excellence. An innovative practice could be a pathway created to further the interest of the student and the institution, for internal quality assurance, inclusive practices and stakeholder relationships.

Key aspects

7.1 Environment Consciousness
7.2 Innovations
7.3 Best Practices

As explained the filling of Self-study report (SSR) for NAAC is not very much different from SAR of NBA. It shall require at least 6 month time of a team of talented faculty member under the leadership of the program coordinator who has long teaching and administrative experience of managing academic activities. One person well versed with the principles of learning and education technology shall be an asset in improving the overall quality of the SSR.

CHAPTER: 9

IAO ACCREDITATION

9.1: About IAO
9.2: Benefits of IAO Accreditation
9.3: IAO's Accreditation Process

9.1 ABOUT IAO

IAO is the short form for International Accreditation Organization. Its headquarters are situated in Huston, Texas, USA (www.iao.org).

IAO is an international quality assurance certification organization, serving to improve quality assurance standards of organizations all over the world. IAO grants accreditation to educational institutions, corporations, professionals and qualified individuals, using its global network of experts and chapters.

Regional accreditation bodies evaluate education service providers on a regional scale and grant to them Primary Accreditation or candidacy certificate. However, the rapid growth of globalization calls for a global entity which can evaluate them against internationally proven standards of education and grant them an internationally recognized Secondary Accreditation. Thus, IAO provides a secondary accreditation certification service, the certification of Regional and National Accreditation Agency of the country should be treated as primary accreditation certification.

IAO enhances the entity's regional/national accreditation and assures stakeholders that the educational program, policies and procedures of the institute, university and school are up to the international standards of quality.

- IAO's International Accreditation represents an education provider's commitment to delivering quality which is on a par with the global standards.
- It assures the stakeholders that their degrees & credits will have increased acceptability around the world, should they decide to study or work abroad.
- The score that an education provider gets under the patented Points Profile System of IAO gives a competitive edge over all regional and international educational institutes, universities and schools.
- IAO's international accreditation for corporations ensures that the organizations are operating according to the international principles and standards of quality. It assures the business community's confidence and trust in your business structure, management & performance.

Additionally, IAO also grants international accreditation to students and professionals for their academic qualifications and professional experience respectively. Being awarded an IAO accreditation holds to it prestige and reputation and the individuals become more desirable partners at global employers, thus getting an opportunity to expand their careers.

9.2: BENEFITS OF IAO ACCREDITATION

- **International Benchmark in Education Standards:** IAO's accreditation ensures that the educational programs of your establishment are easily comparable to any other education provider in any part of the world. IAO's accreditation gives you a competitive edge over all regional and international educational institutions.
- **Academic Support:** IAO's accreditation would cover the courses offered by your prestigious institute, and should you decide to introduce new courses down the line, we would be more than happy to inspect

the material and accredit the courses before they're formally launched so they can have a strong base to start upon.

- **International Acceptability & Promotion:** IAO's accreditation ensures that the degrees and credits of your institution will have increased acceptability around the world by other educational institutions and corporate sector. IAO's accreditation will serve as a platform for International promotion of your institution by IAO's participation in educational events and online educational portals.

- **Affiliation with International University:** IAO's accreditation not only enhances the institute's profile on a regional level but on an International level too, which will result in the collaboration with any international university, that can allow you to have a complete access for student exchange program and also the advance courses adaptation for your university so that your students can also get internationally recognize degrees in their respected field.

- **Tie-up with funding Agency:** To help maintain and enhance your educational standards and practices, IAO will help to provide tie up with the funding agencies in USA who can provide you with foreign funds for the development of your university from all desired aspects.

- **Participation in IAO's Events:** IAO's accreditation will provide an opportunity to your institution's staff members to participate in IAO's conferences and seminars. It will also encourage sharing of information, technology and resources on quality assurance standards and good practices on an international level.

9.3: IAO'S ACCREDITATION PROCESS

For Organizations-Step-1: Similar to any other IAO also pre-recognizes the eligibility of an organization by analyzing its educational programs, resources and processes etc. If the organization satisfies the prequalification criteria of IAO then IAO provides its acceptance certificate that the organization has potential for full accreditation. The benefits of the prequalification certificate is that the institution can use the logo of IAO on its printed academic and managerial/ marketing stationary to attract more talented faculty and students to join their institute and as well retain them for a longer period. This initial step is known as CANDIDACY whose validity period is for 180 days from the date award of certificate of candidacy.

Recently the step may consist of two sub-steps: 1. submission of documents of the institute on-line to the IAO headquarters in USA. 2. Preliminary Inspection of the institute by a member of IAO's Evaluation Commission.

For Organizations-Step2: If the report of the evaluator recommends for full accreditation then after depositing next installment of accreditation fee, full accreditation shall be awarded. However, if the report is not satisfactory, then the institute needs to undertake quality improvement steps wide recommendations of the evaluator and another inspection may be required for verification of the quality status of the institute or program. If all the recommendations have been complied with and the quality status is better than satisfactory the full accreditation certificate shall be awarded after the evaluation report has been accepted by the Evaluation Commission operational at headquarters.

For individuals- Step1: Individual faculty members who are interested in searching and acquiring international recognition may undertake IAO Accredited faculty status may apply for the same by submitting the credentials on-line to IAO.org and then waiting for acceptance letter from IAO which normally should not take more than a fortnight.

For individuals- Step2: Once the Evaluation Commission accepts the credentials, the second step of depositing the requisite fee need to be undertaken. Within a week or so the Status certificate **of "IAO ACCREDITED FACULTY"** certificate shall be issued from IAO, USA.

Empowerment of individual: This certification shall empower the faculty member to get global recognition, having a special page to promote him/herself for global jobs and consultancy assignments etc.

Empowerment of Universities: IAO's accreditation represents university's competence in providing quality education which is on a par with the global standards.

Empowerment of Institutes of higher education: Getting IAO accreditation empowers institute that it is providing a quality education which is recognized all over the world. Institutions can use;

- IAO's Full Accreditation Certificate & Seal:
- Continuous Improvement of your Educational Standards:

Empowerment of Schools: IAO accreditation is proof that your school is committed to providing an education which conforms to international standards. Schools that show deep commitment to enhancing their educational standards and providing exciting student-driven facilities can easily get International Accreditation Organization's reputed accreditation.

- An elementary school offering formal education to children from first to eight years;
- A primary school providing the initial compulsory education, pre-school/nursery education and secondary education;
- A secondary school - intermediate in level between elementary school and college/university;
- A secondary school that offers general, technical, vocational, or college/university - preparatory curricula
- 85% have utilized IAO student services and unleashed numerous career opportunities for their students.

9.4: IAO'S ACCREDITATION CRITERIA

IAO grants international accreditation through a unique and patented **Points Profile System** that is developed by organizing the best global organizational practices in one place in collaboration with regional accreditation bodies. IAO's Point Profile System works as general basis of evaluation for any organization/ individual and provides them with an international accreditation which supplements their regional accreditation. The Points Profile System is a dynamic and evolving system that is continually updated in order to cater to new developments in the academic, business and professional quarters.

There are three major criteria of IAO's accreditation which are briefly explained below:

1. **Organizational Management:** it evaluates the governance and management aspects of the institute or university specifically: vision, mission, Governing Body constitution and its working effectiveness, institutional integrity, policies to manage and deliver services, HR Management and aspects related to Research & scholarship, HR management and marketing efforts etc.

2. **Academic management:** Information about the degree programs offered, Fields of studies, Curriculum Design, flexibility and implementation processes, Admission quality, and credentials and contributions made by its faculty.

3. **Institutional Performance:** Aspects related to accomplishments of alumni and their connectivity with the organization, assessment system to measure Students' performance, and accreditation of the organization by other relevant national or regional agencies

The evaluators visit to different departments and divisions of the organizations and try to assess the performance against all criteria mentioned above and prepare a report in a detailed format consisting of a number of pages. The organization is also asked to prepare a self-assessment report on a similar format and try verify the contents of different statements made in the self-assessment report. It takes minimum one day to complete the inspection of a normal Institute or a school; however it may take about two days for inspection of a large university.

I personally recommend that every university and an educational institute/school should undertake IAO's accreditation as a secondary accreditation certification. Regional and national accreditation certification along with IAO's certification will make any educational enterprise proud to earn the following benefits: Global recognition and global propagation of its brand image. It shall help in attracting the best national and international students and faculty members who will further improve the future prospects of success of the enterprise due to their individual talents and credentials. Although, it shall invite more efforts and investments in the beginning, but the rate of returns on investments will surely be increasing with time and normal improvements in quality of delivery as well as word of mouth based branding of the enterprise.

SELECTED REFERENCES FOR FURTHER STUDY

A: Different information available on general websites
- http://en.wikipedia.org/wiki/Economy
- Unesco Report 2002: Trade in Higher education Services, The Implications of GATS
- http://www.unesco.org/education/studyingabroad/highlights/globalforum/gats_he/jk_trade_he_gats_implications.pdf, Pub March 2002
- http://nbaind.org/En/1033-washington-accord.aspx#sthash.klAu6YQ0.dpuf
- Engg Council UK: http://www.engc.org.uk/education--skills/international-recognition-agreements
- International Engg Alliance: http://www.ieagreements.org/
- http://en.wikipedia.org/wiki/Economy_of_India
- http://www.aicte-india.org/aboutaicte.htm
- http://en.wikipedia.org/wiki/Quality_assurance
- http://edcilindia.co.in/
- http://epltt.coe.uga.edu/index.php?title=Adult_Learning
- http://www.mindtools.com/pages/article/worksheets/SWOTAnalysisWorksheet.pdf
- http://www.ganttproject.biz/
- http://www.iitd.ac.in/content/vision-mission-values
- www.ssgmce.org

- ROLE OF WASHINGTON ACCORD ON ACCREDITATION- Prof BC Majumder, www.nitttrbhopal.org/ index.php?option=com_docman&task... Seminar on "Washington Accord: India's Preparedness" at NITTR, Bhopal on January 6 and 7, 2011\
- http://www.abet.org/engineering-technology-mra-dublin-accord/
- http://www.ieagreements.org/IEA-Grad-Attr-Prof-Competencies.pdf
- PIP of TEQIP-II, Version 2009, http://www.npiu.nic.in/
- http://en.wikipedia.org/wiki/Autonomy
- http://en.wikipedia.org/wiki/Assessment_for_Learning
- http://www.ehow.com/facts_5929463_assessment-learning_.html
- http://www.washingtonaccord.org/IEA-Grad-Attr-Prof-Competencies.pdf
- {Policy Forum No. 20: Accreditation and global higher education market http://www.iiep.unesco.org/fileadmin/user_upload/Info_Services_Publications/pdf/2008/PolForum_20.pdf}
- Standards and Guidelines for Quality Assurance in the European: Higher Education Area
- http://en.wikipedia.org/wiki/List_of_recognized_higher_education_accreditation_organizations

PB: Specific Guidelines & Manuals related to Accreditation available on the relevant websites given below:

- NBA, India: www.nbaind.org
- NAAC, India: www.naac.gov.in
- AICTE, India: www.aicte-india.org
- UGC, India: www.ugc.ac.in
- Ministry of Human Resources Development, India: www.mhrd.gov.in

Epilogue

This is the first edition of the book of its own class. Most of the content has been developed on the bases of the practice based experience and inference drawn during the discussions held with talented faculty members belonging to different technical Colleges spread all over India. The surrounding countries shall be using similar accreditation criteria and approach by their national regulatory bodies and the approach used in India under Washington accord should be applicable in almost all countries which have become provisional signatories of Washington Accord (Srilanka, Pakistan, and Bangladesh)

Consultants generally hesitate in sharing their experience based trade secrets & insight with the fraternity of Professional faculty members and sometimes such valuable information gets lost. My desire to publish such a book from a very reputed publishing house is to reach out the widest possible fraternity of higher technical education in the developing countries who might be requiring a few hints on the subject and rest they shall apply their own expertise to complete the task of making quality documents or Self-assessment reports etc. which shall be accepted by the regulatory bodies and acquiring accreditation of their quality assurance endeavors becomes a simpler process. I am sure with time and more experience with outcome based educational accreditation certifications, the contents and presentations of the book can be improved a lot.

I, therefore, request the users of the book to kindly send their suggestions and valuable feedback for enriching subsequent editions of the book at my e-mail address: satishksoni@outlook.com. These suggestions will go a long way in improving the information and guidelines for the future users of the book and improving the quality assurance practices in the higher professional education in Indian sub-continent and other developing countries of the world.

I hope my investment on self-publishing of the book shall facilitate accreditation of many professional technical institutions and universities.

Prof Satish Kumar Soni, May, 2014,
Website: www.nba-accreditation-consultancy.in, e-mail: satishksoni@ outlook.com, Linkedin URL: http://www.linkedin.com/profile/ view?id=15473068&trk=nav_ responsive_tab_profile, Cell: +91 9303124944

About the author

The author is a retired Professor from NITTTR, Bhopal, MP, India (BE-IIT-BHU-Varanasi, UP, 1966 & ME-MNIT-Allahabad-UP, 1971). He has been pursuing Quality Improvement and Assurance practices for last 25 years. He was trained in UK and USA in application of Education Technology. Currently, he is doing consultancy for accreditation of Professional programs and institutions since 2012.

He has guided 3 PhD research scholars in the area of Technical education and quality Improvement who are working as dean and HoDs in National Institute of Technical Teachers Training and Research, Bhopal, India. As a Mechanical Engineer he undertook a challanging Project of Developing a broadcast quality TV Studion during 1984 to 1989 and produced a large number of electronic media based learning resources like Video Programs and multimmedia self-learning packages.The author has been contributing to quality assurance projects funded by global development agencies for last 25 years. He is still very active at the age of 72+.